The Travels of a Shepherd Boy

Ogilvie Dickson

Printed by Buccleuch Printers Limited, Carnarvon Street, Hawick

Edited and published by Ogilvie Dickson
St John's Cottage
Huntly Avenue, Melrose, Roxburghshire TD6 9SD
T: 01896 820038

Travels of a Shepherd Boy may be obtained from Ogilvie Dickson at the above address.

First published 2007

Contents

Introduction

I am indeed proud and privileged to have been born into a loving, caring and very strict Presbyterian family, who provided a firm foundation on how to live a fulfilling and meaningful life, hopefully enriching the lives of others.

As we travel along life's pathways, one certainly encounters challenges and it is therefore important to align oneself to one's unique pathway, which could lead to a radically different life from others.

We all have a choice . . .

We cannot always be the best, but we should always try our best!

Henry Ford once said . . .

There isn't a person anywhere who isn't capable of doing more than he thinks he can!

I have tried . . .

Foreword

It is said that there is no finer place in which to start life than in a shepherd's cottage. Ogilvie Dickson's story proves the truth of this saying.

He was born in 1937 in the Roughley Cottage, which overlooks Hermitage Castle in Liddesdale. His father was the highly respected shepherd at Shaws farm, which in those days was run by Mr Ballantyne, whose family had come from Peebleshire in 1823 to take up the tenancy on the Buccleuch Estate.

Mr Dickson describes a strict but happy childhood in the remote cottage, which had no electricity or road access, and where the door was never locked. Schooling, first Hermitage, then at Newcastleton and Selkirk, was not a great success, although he made many lifelong friends.

He left at the age of nearly 15, having persuaded the headmaster that his time would be better spent among sheep.

A strong entrepreneurial streak had already shown itself. Ogilvie was rearing ducks and trapping moles for a profit when still a boy. National Service with the KOSB in Malaya opened windows on a wider world and gave him a lifelong love of travel, as well as enormous respect for the Gurkhas with whom he served.

From then on nothing could stop Ogilvie Dickson. Read this book, and you will see how much it is possible to pack in to one mortal span given energy, talent, ambition and above all that 'can do' attitude that regards every problem as an opportunity and, by looking for the silver lining, succeeds in finding it.

Emma Tennant
January 2007

Acknowledgements

John and Roselle Boyd Brent, Aboutscotland.com.

Angus Blackburn, Photographer.

George and Margaret Borthwick, Edinburgh.

Robert D Clapperton, Photographic Trust, Selkirk.

Jake Coltman, Stamp Historian, Hawick.

Paul Dickson, Peebles.

Eskdale & Liddesdale Advertiser, Langholm.

Alasdair Fletcher, Editor of The Scottish Farmer, Glasgow.

John Fraser, Chief Photographer, The Scottish Farmer, for providing the front cover.

The Farmer and Stock Breeder, Preston.

The Gurkha Welfare Trust, London.

The Thomas Hope Hospital, Langholm.

Historic Scotland, Edinburgh.

Atholl Innes, Editor, The Border Telegraph, Galashiels.

Wing Commander (Rtd) David Jones.

Vanessa Jordan Photography, Galway, Ireland.

John Lewis plc.

Lewis Photos Limited, London.

Catherine A Macgregor Photography, Kilsyth, for providing the back cover.

Malaysia Airlines.

Mick Murphy, Publisher Freighter Travel Review.

Davie McCrindle, Kirkmahoe, Dumfries.

Major John Patchett, Kingussie.

National Museum of Singapore.

David D Stevenson, Langholm.

Susan Windram, Editor, The Southern Reporter, Selkirk.

Scottish Borders Council.

I am most grateful to the above firms and individuals for their enthusiastic support
and co-operation with the production of this book.

I would especially like to thank Lady Emma Tennant of Shaws, Newcastleton for writing the Foreword.

Chapter 1 – Arriving in this Wonderful World

All the family meals were cooked on this open fire (the body of the fire has been replaced in recent times).

On the 14th March 1937, after an urgent message was received in Stichill village north of Kelso, nurse Davidson quickly bundled some personal belongings into a bag and made her way to Kelso Station, for a steam train to Hawick. Changing to the Waverley Line, she arrived at the remote Steel Road Station, South of Whitrope Tunnel, to be met by David Ballantyne, Farmer of Shaws Farm in Liddesdale.

Quickly donning her 'welly' boots at the farm, she made her way through knee-high snow drifts up the hillside to Roughley, the shepherd's cottage on Shaws Farm, nestling at the foothills of Arnton Fell.

Here on the morning of the 15th March 1937, she helped to deliver me into this wonderful world. Rearing brother Jimmie, sister Frances and now an addition must have been tough for my mother, with no radio, television, electric light, central heating, and all food and house supplies to be carried over a mile from the nearest public road, apart from the annual supply of 1cwt of flour, 1cwt of oatmeal, plus a few cartloads of coal, with father supplementing the fuel supply with hand-sawn logs when time would permit.

With father's meagre earnings, subsistence, recycling and resourcefulness were the order of the day. The vegetables from a huge garden, mother's bannocks and rhubarb tarts, milk from our own cow, eggs from our hens with the odd cockerel for the pot plus the demise of our friendly pig, kept us sustained for each long 12 months. Nothing was thrown away: Weetabix outer cartons were my drums, with hazel drumsticks plucked from a bush. Clothes were all recycled and even our henhouses were constructed by father from recycled wood.

During the long winter evenings illumination would be provided by Tilley paraffin lamps, and when the paraffin supply was exhausted, candles would take their place.

Father would use a recycled, washed ex-animal feed hessian sack stretched over a wooden frame, to produce rag rugs from strips of old clothes. Whilst mother knitted our socks, father knitted our gloves and the haircuts he gave us were of the highest order. He even re-modelled my mother's hats for special occasions.

The door was always unlocked until the war years, when father had to trudge through the hills for duties in the dugout of the local Observation Corps, near Steel Road, and listen helplessly to the drone of German bombers on their way to bomb Clydebank.

The Roughley, my birthplace. Greatmoor (once a volcano) is on the left, and on the right the two-mile track to the then roadless Riccarton Junction

Photograph by John Boyd Brent, Aboutscotland.com

Hermitage Schooldays (1942-1949)

I was introduced to Hermitage School when I was five years of age and during the 1940's we had some of the hardest winters on record. In snow storms father would pull a 'one man snow plough' over a mile to ensure our attendance at school! My first recollection of my days at Hermitage School was the arrival of a nice young teacher by the name of Miss Hampton. In our naivety we were all so curious as to why she would rush off on her bicycle at lunchtime, heading for Hermitage Castle. We soon discovered 'this was no history lesson' but a meeting with her boyfriend, John Scott of Gorrenberry, whom she eventually married. Our lunchtimes were spent 'guddling' eels in the Hermitage River in lovely sunshine. It always appeared to be sunny during the summer as children. On hearing about the arrival of our new headteacher, we were apprehensive as we heard she was coming from that very far-off land The Hebrides. In fact, she came from Lochmaddy. (Little did I think that one day I would build the new auction mart at Lochmaddy and have it inspected by Prince Charles and Diana.)

Mrs McLachlan was a true Highlander, strict on religion but not arithmetic. I can recall having four sums on my slate for a full week and when she approached me I would re-write them with no input from her whatsoever. Mrs McLachlan was not the most intellectually inspiring teacher, but what she did was to teach us to differentiate between right and wrong. I can still vividly remember the distinct smell from the coke burning stove, which formed the centre piece at the front of the classroom. Mrs McLachlan would stand with her back to the stove, and clean out her ears with a hairpin with the hard yellow wax cascading to the floor!

Attending Hermitage School during the war years saw considerable military activity in the area, with visits to Beating Retreat in Newcastleton, courtesy of Farmer Tom Scott of the Dinley. As a child, one expected German soldiers to arrive in the valley at any time! There was great excitement on the day that a crashed Spitfire was towed by two Clydesdale horses from the adjoining Toftholm Hill to the main road. Attending Hermitage School was a very carefree period, unfortunately with minimal educational input, but with friendships made that have survived for over 65 years.

Life at Roughley during my formative years left an indelible mark on my memory. We had a very strict regime willingly accepted: no gramophone, music, football or the washing of clothes on a Sunday. Weather permitting, we would make an eight mile round trip by bicycle to the rear pew in Castleton Church.

On the first Sunday in August, with a pocketful of gooseberries to sustain us over a five mile walk we made our way to Hermitage Castle for the annual open air service!

Father was always industrious and supportive and spent a great deal of his time helping others. He was the secretary of 'The Liddesdale Cow Club', a specialist locally organised insurance for cottagers' cows, which were inspected for health prior to acceptance. The 10/- (50p) annual premium assisted in providing a pay-out should a cottager lose his cow.

On occasions, father would take us on a day out to collect supplies from Hawick. This entailed a four mile walk to and from Riccarton Junction (a substantial village of 34 houses built in Victorian times and demolished after the Beeching axe). It was accessed only by rail. We would leave our wooden soled clogs or wellies at the station and change into shoes for the train journey to Hawick. Father was not averse to visiting Tom Middlemass the scrap merchant who always had a good selection of recycled tools, and Jimmie Lamb to collect his seeds for his huge garden. One entire wall of the shop was formed with small drawers full of bulk seed, which were carefully weighed into packets. I can still clearly recall the day he brought home our very first radio, a Raymond portable dry battery model and a friend who gave me one of Mr Biro's very first ball point pens!

My entrepreneurial spirit was about to take root with my very first wage of a glossy white Bank of England £5 note at the age of 12 (a fortune for a schoolboy then). This was earned by assisting father at lambing time and proved to be a huge incentive. I then embarked on duck rearing for a profit and the trapping of moles. At one point I could earn 2/6 (12.5p) per dried mole pelt.

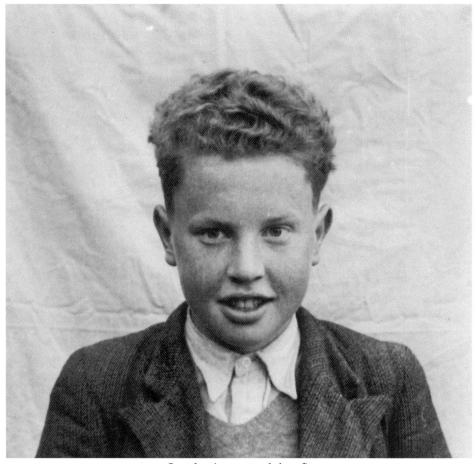

Complete in my recycled outfit.

Newcastleton Village School

Photography by Ogilvie Dickson

Off to Newcastleton Secondary School

With my primary education doubtful, I found secondary education difficult, with algebra and geometry incomprehensible. By the time I was 13½ Father and Mother moved to Selkirkshire where I had yet another school move, to Selkirk High School, where at the age of 14 years 11 months I requested a meeting with Mr Kennedy, the Rector. I put it to him that my time would be better spent among sheep than in his classroom and I was relieved when he agreed!

The Shaws Clipping (Shearing)
4th July 1947

Lambing and clipping (shearing) were my favourite times in the sheep calendar. I was always amazed when each year prior to lambing, a large bottle of gin appeared from my father's boss Mr Ballantyne. This was certainly not to sustain father during a busy period, but to prescribe to lambs with hypothermia!

Before leaving school, the Shaws clipping was a day I always wished to have off school but without success. However, immediately after school, I was among the clippers (shearers), listening to the banter at what was really a social event, with neighbouring farmers and estate gamekeepers joining in.

Back Row: Robbie Forster, Andy Knox, Polish Gentleman, Billy Currie, Jock Elliot.
Middle Row: Jock Cowan, John Nichol, Self, John Waugh, Eddie Nixon, Mr Shillinglaw, George Aitchison, Jim Wallace.
Front Row: Brother Jimmie, Jim Murray, Tommy Crozier, David Ballantyne, Tom Elliot, Father.

Billy Currie, Mr Shillinglaw, Brother Jimmie with Father in the distance.

At the ready with my marking iron used with marking fluid and applied to identify each farm's flock of sheep by their own initials.

Hermitage

The original Schoolhouse, School and Hermitage Hall

Hermitage School Reunion 9th October 2005

Reunions are always difficult to organise and, as the school closed its doors on the 3rd of July 1952, it was a great credit to Joyce Forster for being able to recruit so many from yesteryear.

Joyce was assisted by her mother and Aunts Nellie and Jean Anderson (now Nellie Byers and Jean Mitchison) with additional assistance from Jean Currie (now Jean Graham) and Jean Elliot from Newcastleton.

Hermitage Castle: a remarkable fortress

Hermitage Castle is a property in the care of Historic Scotland
Crown Copyright. Published with the permission of Historic Scotland

My photographs above of Hermitage Castle are of that magnificent stronghold, which I would gaze at across the valley each morning from Roughley and admire. I have also included a picture of the display board at the castle entrance which clearly indicates the previous notoriety of the valley of my birth.

Chapter 2 – My Family

DICKSON

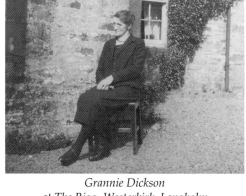

My Father

With my sister, Frances, and brother, Jimmie.

My Mother

Grandpa Dickson

*Grannie Dickson
at The Rigg, Westerkirk, Langholm*

*Grandpa Scott with part of the family and Grannie Scott (nee Margaret Ogilvie)
whose family came down from the North and farmed Middlemoss, near Langholm.
My mother is in the front of the photograph on the right,
taken at Saughtree, Liddesdale.*

Ogilvie tartan

MIDDLETON

Flora's Father

John, Jean and Flora

Flora's Mother

Grandpa Middleton, Fraserburgh

Grannie Middleton, Fraserburgh

Grandpa MacDonald, Isle of Bute
Served in the Boer war 1901-1902 as a private in the medical corps.
Attached to the 107 Co Imperial Yeomanry, Army number 29859

Grannie MacDonald, Isle of Bute

The Flying Scotsman

Son Jim has always been a two-wheel enthusiast and now takes his mountain bikes all over the world, competing in the most arduous mountain bike events on the calendar. These include cycling from Machu Picchu to the Amazon Basin, through part of the Rockies, a week's marathon along the Garden Route in Southern Africa and in Europe, through part of Poland. Here he is, competing in his home territory on one of the sport's most successful tracks in Peeblesshire.

When not mountain biking, he is an oil industry Engineering Manager, having helped to extend Singapore's refinery and Laem Chabang refinery in Thailand.

We warmly welcome a new member to our family, Dympna, Jim's lovely wife from Galway, that delightful part of Southern Ireland. Here they are in Galway Bay on their wedding day.

My Family

EWM proves its ahead of the field in Malaysia Games

When Scotland's Commonwealth Games team takes to the track in Malaysia next year there will be more than a passing interest for Langholmites.

For the team will be kitted out in uniforms specially designed at Edinburgh Woollen Mill's Waverley Mill in the town.

While the company has been involved in the design since its Chairman David Stevenson was one of the team members back in 1970, this will be a first in the way the design has been chosen.

For this year they have given two young design students the opportunity to make their mark on the international scene.

Flora Dickson and Victoria Sinclair won the opportunity of a lifetime through an assignment to come up with designs for the Scottish team as part of their BSc course in clothing design and manufacture.

The two are students at the Scottish College of Textiles in Galashiels and also won cash prizes and the opportunity to meet the Games Team next year.

Mr Stevenson says he is delighted with the project.

"It's great for us to be able to support the Scottish Team in this traditional way while at the same time giving exciting new Scottish designers the chance to turn their ideas into finished outfits."

As part of their prize the girls have been taken on for six month work placements with EWM during which time they are able to work on the designs for the Games under the skilled supervision of EWM's own designers.

The uniforms will represent style and quality synonymous with the company's heritage whilst using colourful, lively designs reflecting the Kuala Lumpur official hibiscus flower logo.

For all the Games uniforms EWM based its designs on the colours of the country, the logo and Scottish tartan, although it has given them some problems on occasions, particularly when one year the main colour was black with a just little gold, says Mr Stevenson.

But for at least another month the designs are being kept under wraps.

David Stevenson takes a look at some of Flora's designs as Victoria looks on

Daughter Flora modelling for John Lewis plc in Princes Street Gardens Edinburgh

We warmly welcome a new member to our family, Flora's husband Mark, Managing Director, Grosvenor Farms, Cheshire.

BORDER TELEGRAPH

GALASHIELS, TUESDAY, JULY 27, 1982

Galashiels housewife graduates

LAST Saturday was a very important day for Flora Dickson, Wylies Brae, Galashiels, when she graduated Bachelor of Science at Edinburgh University.

To most students university involves total devotion to studies and residing close to university, but not for 41-year-old Flora.

To study for her three-year degree course in Engineering Science at Edinburgh meant an early morning call—breakfast with her two children, Flora 17 and Jim 16, before they left for Galashiels Academy, and then the morning drive to Edinburgh and a day's work at the university, home to provide tea for the whole family, then more studying often into the early hours of the morning.

In common with so many potential students, Flora did not have the opportunity of a university course in her teens. So when the Open University came along she applied in 1971 for a place and obtained a B.A. in 1978 after seven years of studies at home which allowed her to look after the family. In 1977 she also sat the O.N.C. course in Building at Galashiels College of Further Education and passed with distinction.

A person of many parts, she still finds time to be a director of her husband's Farm Building Company, membership of the Scottish Solar Energy Group, membership of the Energy Committee of the Society's Religion and Technology Project of the Church of Scotland.

Flora, my loving wife for over 40 years.

No pet dog or pussy cat for the Dickson family, but a lamb that grew into a sheep!

Here young Flora and Jim take 'Blackie' for a stroll in Galashiels High Street!

S.S. Caledonia, 1904, Anchor Line.

Great Uncle Thomas Dickson took 9 weeks to reach New York on this ship, when he emigrated to America in 1910. He died in 1926.

Hawick's earliest known postmarked letter.

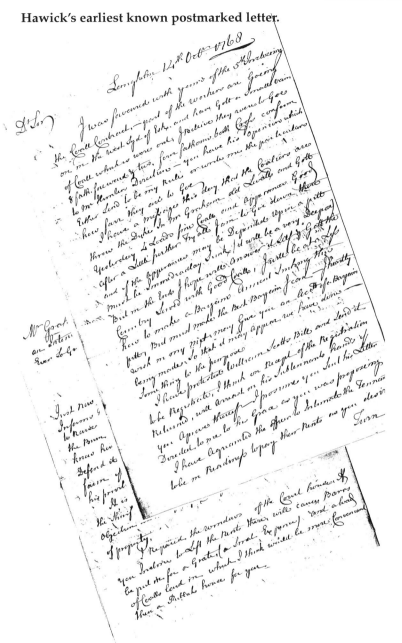

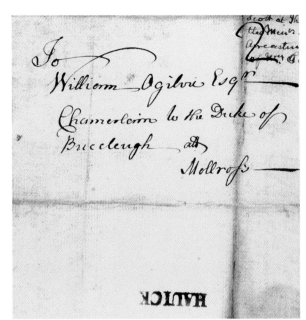

Hawick's earliest known postmarked letter?

A letter has been acquired by local postal history collector Jake Coltman which is thought to be the earliest known item bearing a Hawick postmark.

The official post in Hawick was established on 5th July 1768. The letter in question is dated 14th October of that year. According to records at Hawick Museum, the earliest item is 1770, which is contained in their small postal history collection.

The 1768 letter was sent by a Matthew Little, Langholm, and addressed to William Ogilvie, Chamberlain to the Duke of Buccleugh (note: g), Mellross (again note the spelling of Melrose). The letter contains numerous other spelling anomalies as goe, farr, coall, syd, gott, mixt, pitt and barrs, which are quite common for this time. The letter is postmarked HAUICK (again note the spelling), this being the nearest post town to Langholm at the time. The charge of 2d, shown in manuscript on the front, was the basic rate for up to 50 miles.

In the letter, Mr Little acknowledges receipt of a "coall contract" and informs the Duke's Chamberlain of the progress of the Canonbie Coal Co., of which His Grace was the owner.

A mining of considerable importance to the locality was situated at Canonbie. Borings for coal were made with such success that in 1792 at a depth of 68 feet a seam was found two feet thick and, at a depth of 146 feet, another seam five feet eight inches thick was discovered. Operations were on such a scale that supplying this invaluable commodity for industrial and household purposes was not confined to the Border area but also farther afield.

The mining of coal brought with it many improvements in the area, the most notable being a railway and the construction of better roads. Because of the mines, the Duke of Buccleuch was able to present a strong and, in the end, successful case for the Carlisle to Edinburgh railway line to be routed via Canonbie, leaving Langholm to be served by a branch line.

Operations at Canonbie ceased at the turn of this century. In the closing years the coalfields produced approximately 18,000 tons annually and found employment for over 100 men and boys at any one time.

Coming back to the letter, it was during the early years of Hawick's postal history that incoming letters were placed on a stall in the street on market days and even on the tombstones in St Mary's Churchyard and, according to reports, "like so many cakes of gingerbread." People used to look at them with curiosity. In those days a letter writer used one sheet of paper which was subsequently folded, addressed on the front and the flaps sealed.

One of my ancestors, William Ogilvie, had the distinction of receiving one of the very first letters bearing a Hawick postmark. Since the above article was printed further research has revealed that the first recorded letter was 26th July 1768. However, given that there would not be much mail, William Ogilvie's letter has to be one of the earliest.

Fifth Generation

Francis Dickson was born in 1779 in Ewes, Dumfriesshire. He died on 14 December 1820 in Southdeanriggshiel, Teviothead. He was buried in Teviothead Kirkyard.

Appears on Ewes Militia List for 1802 call up in the event of Napoleon invading.

Isabella Hope 1825-1898

JULY 21, 1994
100 Years Ago
The Hope Trustees met on Saturday to receive the report of the assessing architect, Mr Christian, of the five competitive plans for the proposed Hospital, and they resolved to accept the design sent in by Mr Wood, New Bond Street, London, and to lose no time in taking the necessary steps for proceeding with the building.

From the E&L files

Thomas Hope 1809-1890

When I was visiting Roy and Pat Grieve, my cousins in the Okanagan Valley in British Columbia, I was intrigued by the old faded picture on the wall. I soon discovered it was Isabella Hope, my Great Grandmother. She had an uncle called Thomas Hope and as I delved deeper, a fascinating story gradually unfolded.

Thomas Hope's father, Matthew Hope, had a cotton mill in Langholm which was not successful. His mother was Grace Corrie from near Lockerbie. In 1817, the father and son James emigrated to New York and two years later the mother and the rest of the children, including Thomas, joined them on a voyage of about nine weeks. Owing to their financial circumstances their school fees were left unpaid on leaving Langholm.

Many years later when Thomas Hope returned a wealthy man, he contacted the schoolmaster and more than repaid him.

Thomas Hope and his brother started a small grocery store in New York which developed

into a huge business empire of 30 stores, in various parts of the country.

On retirement and on his visit of 1888, he made public his most generous offer of the erection and maintenance of a home in Langholm for the aged and infirm natives of the district, to be called 'The Thomas Hope Hospital'.

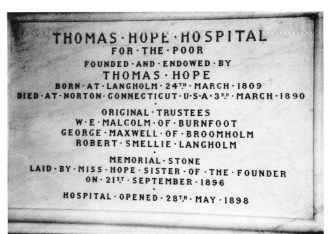

THOMAS · HOPE · HOSPITAL
FOR · THE · POOR
FOUNDED · AND · ENDOWED · BY
THOMAS · HOPE
BORN · AT · LANGHOLM · 24TH · MARCH · 1809
DIED · AT · NORTON · CONNECTICUT · U·S·A · 3RD · MARCH · 1890

ORIGINAL · TRUSTEES
W·E · MALCOLM · OF · BURNFOOT
GEORGE · MAXWELL · OF · BROOMHOLM
ROBERT · SMELLIE · LANGHOLM

MEMORIAL · STONE
LAID · BY · MISS · HOPE · SISTER · OF · THE · FOUNDER
ON · 21ST · SEPTEMBER · 1896

HOSPITAL · OPENED · 28TH · MAY · 1898

Chapter 3 – National Service

The KOSB Depot, Berwick-upon-Tweed
5 January to 16 March 1956

These Border men took part in the passing out parade at the KOSB Depot at Berwick

They are: Standing, left to right; J. Turner, Galashiels; J. Nichol, Newcastleton; W. Mabon, Gordon; A. Dickie, Selkirk; J. Wilson, Kelso;
T. Sadler, Jedburgh; J. Mabon, Kelso; M. Adamson, Newcastleton.
Sitting, left to right; N. Yule, Earlston; R. Scott, Langholm; R. Gilligan, Hawick; O. Dickson, Selkirk; D. Thomson, Melrose.

I Volunteer for National Service.
After three years' practical farming (sheep, cattle and arable) one wet harvest helped persuade me that a change in direction was inevitable. Whilst in employment of His Grace The Duke of Buccleuch, his factor, a fine gentleman, the Hon James Galbraith, assured me that if I remained in agriculture I would be exempt from National Service. I thanked him for his offer but confirmed that I would volunteer. I was immediately drafted to the King's Own Scottish Borderers at Berwick and, within weeks, I was on my way by air to join the 1st Battalion KOSB in Singapore.

On 18th April 1956 I left Lyneham Airport, Wiltshire, on a four-day flight to Singapore in a Hermes Prop Aircraft. After a few weeks in Selerang Garrison near Changi to allow a brief period of acclimatization, we were on our way to the Battalion Head Quarters at Batu Pahat Johore, Malaya.

AW 184/312

FLIGHT SCHEDULE.

UK - - - - - SINGAPORE

		hrs GMT		hrs LOCAL		
	Depart	1015 hrs GMT	1015 hrs LOCAL	1st Day
BRINDISI	Arrive	1630 " "	1730 " "	"
BRINDISI	Depart	1745 " "	1845 " "	"
BEIRUT LEBANON	Arrive	2310 " "	0110 " "	"
BEIRUT	Depart	0045 " "	0245 " "	2nd Day
BAHREIN	Arrive	0555 " "	0855 " "	"
BAHREIN	Depart	0710 " "	1010 " "	"
KARACHI	Arrive	1210 " "	1710 " "	"
NIGHT STOP				
KARACHI	Depart	0340 " "	0840 " "	3rd Day
DELHI	Arrive	0700 " "	1230 " "	"
DELHI	Depart	0815 " "	1405 " "	"
CALCUTTA	Arrive	1215 " "	1745 " "	"
NIGHT STOP				
CALCUTTA	Depart	0001 " "	0531 " "	4th Day
BANGKOK	Arrive	0500 " "	1200 " "	"
BANGKOK	Depart	0615 " "	1315 " "	"
SINGAPORE	Arrive	1050 " "	1820 " "	"
(PAYA LEBAR AIRPORT)				

Our actual flight schedule of 50 years ago.

The vehicle that was to change my life.

I scrubbed and polished my jeep with great vigour, which didn't go unnoticed by the Motor Transport Officer who called me into his office and asked if I would be interested in being staff car driver to the 63rd Gurkha Infantry Brigade Commander, J S Vickers DSO. I just couldn't believe that for the first time in my army service, I was being asked, not told; however, I immediately agreed!

From a timid country boy I had to change dramatically and use my own initiative, think on my feet and deal with ADC's to four-star generals, which greatly assisted me both in the army and beyond . . .

My jeep at Batu Pahat, Johore, Malaya

My escort for 18,362 miles in Malaya (1956-1958). Gurkha Tam Ding Sherpa from Janakapur, East Nepal, with his Rolls-Royce engined armoured Ferret car with Browning machine gun.

Not only had I a reliable Gurkha escort, but also shared a camp with these fine soldiers from the hills of Nepal. One was a fellow driver who became a good friend. I discovered he had two wives (perfectly legal in Nepal). I challenged Purnasing by asking, 'How do you cope with two wives?' 'No problem Sahib' came the quick reply, 'I sleep in the middle!'

DROVE PRINCE IN MALAYA

During the recent visit to Malaya of H.R.H. The Duchess of Gloucester, and Prince William, a Selkirk man had the honour of driving the young prince during part of the visit. He is Lance Corporal Ogilvie Dickson, whose parents live at "Newarkburn," Bowhill, Selkirk.

L/Cpl. Dickson is pictured in front of the staff car in which he drove Prince William when their Highnesses visited the 1st Battalion, The King's Own Scottish Borderers, in South Malaya.

A National Serviceman, L/Cpl. Dickson's usual job is staff car driver to his Brigade Commander—Brigadier J. S. Vickers, D.S.O.

From the flight deck of Britain's very first passenger jet aircraft, the Comet.

Sitting on the tarmac at Bahrain, where we had an overnight stop, was our sleek new Comet jet from De Haviland.

R.A.F. Form 1256F.

TRANSPORT COMMAND

R. A. F.

To PASSENGERS   **PLEASE PASS ROUND**

From CAPTAIN S/L HARPER

Time 0105   Aircraft 715

G.M.T. 0635   Local Time

Our position is 190 mm SW of CAR NICOBAR

Altitude 40,500 feet. Temperature -58 deg. Cent.

Ground Speed 504 miles per hour.

Our Flight Plan estimated a 03 hrs. 53 mins. Flight.

We are hrs. ON mins. ahead of / behind Schedule.

Our estimated time of arrival at KATUNAYAKA

is 0253 G.M.T. 0825 Local Time.

In mins. we should pass on our Starboard / Port

NOTHING UNTIL CEYLON

Remarks :

(•135) Wt. 17513—883 10M Pads 8/50 T.S. 839

Navigator.

Heading for Ceylon (now Sri Lanka) on our two-day trip home by Comet, cutting 50% off the outward journey.

Chapter 4 – My Businesses

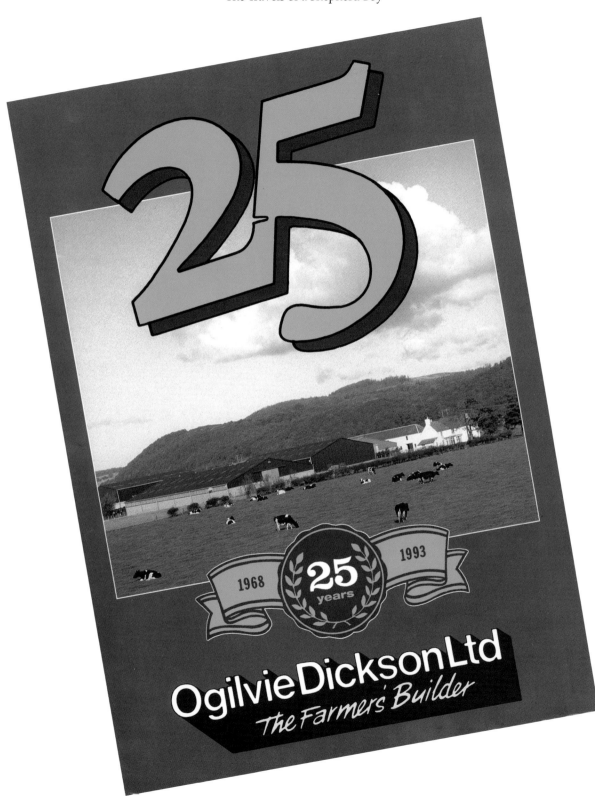

W.N. PON - KOEPON
Antumerweg 5
9893 TA Garnwerd Nederland
telefoon 05941-1696
fax   05941-1610
ABN-Amrobank 48.53.64.476

Ogilvie Dickson Limited
Attn.: Mr. O. Dickson
85 Queen Street
Galashiels TD1 1QF
Scotland

Date: March 30, 1993
Ref.: 930347/WNP/eW

Dear Mr. Dickson,

Congratulations with your 25th Anniversary of your company!

I am glad that you did a great job for us and I am proud to be at the cover of your brochure.

Wishing you all the best for the future, I remain,

with best regards,
W.N. PON — KOEPON

W.N. Pon

cc.: J. Vos, Coopon Carse

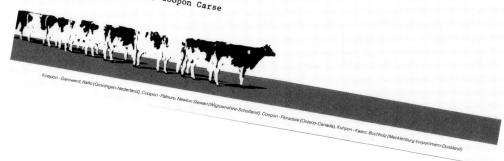

Koepon - Garnwerd, Baflo (Groningen-Nederland), Coopon - Palnure, Newton Stewart (Wiglownshire-Schotland), Coopon - Floradale (Ontario-Canada), Kuhpon - Kaarz, Buchholz (Mecklenburg Vorpommern-Duitsland)

On completion of National Service, I returned to a severe recession. I refused unemployment benefit and, to survive, I planted and felled trees, drove trucks and tractors and was a dustman for a day.

I then joined a builder and gained valuable building and excavator operator's experience. However, I decided selling was the direction I should be heading, and after many interviews I was successful in being appointed a trainee salesman with Levers Feeds, part of the huge Unilever Group.

I was given an area in the South West of Scotland with virtually no existing business, so times were tough, payment was by straight commission only, so I gave Flora, my wife, £5 per week for food and to keep our new home and a further £5 per week was allocated to the running costs of my Morris Minor car.

I would take sandwiches with me on my daily calls round the farms, and an axe, an unusual combination!

The sandwiches were for sustenance and the axe to chop firewood from old branches on the side of the country roads at lunchtime. With our frugal existence and hard work, I paid off our mortgage in two years and became the top company salesman in Scotland, with the inevitable promotion to Area Manager for the South of Scotland, which did not appeal to me. I left after eight years and soon took the brave decision to borrow (which at that time appeared to be a huge sum of money) and start my own construction company.

In Lochfoot Road, Kirkcudbrightshire

Pioneer of package-deal farm building contracts.

I introduced a completely new farm building service, well aware of the difficulty encountered by farmers planning a new building, where companies were keen to supply and erect a frame and leave the client the often mammoth and time-consuming task of organising plant contractors, builders, plumbers and electricians. I realised here was a market ready for development and it is true to say Ogilvie Dickson pioneered 'Package-Deal' farm building contracts in Scotland and further afield!

During 26 years in construction I experienced a builder's strike, telephone strike, cement strike, petrol strike and postal strike. I found the postal strike the most difficult because it involved having to drive to Kendal to rendezvous with my southern supplier to exchange mail.

Petrol ration book and coupon issued during the petrol strike of 1973.

NEWS PAGE

Royal Visit

I was honoured by a visit to our new Mart building at Lochmaddy by the Prince and Princess of Wales whilst on their historic Hebridean Tour.

SOUTH OF SCOTLAND FARM BUILDING AWARD WINNER 1986

With over 20 years' experience in sheep housing Ogilvie Dickson probably has more knowledge than most in this rapidly developing market.

We were delighted with winning the very first South of Scotland Farm Buildings Award for the 380' x 60' sheep house erected near Stirling which will house 1000 grey faced ewes in a well designed and well ventilated building.

Loading some of the crates at Galashiels for shipment to the Falklands contract.

FALKLANDS TRIUMPH

One of the real feathers in our cap in recent times has been our involvement in the supply of the new Dairy Buildings and equipment to Ross Dairy at Stanley on the Falkland Islands, South Atlantic.

The contract was won under intense competition from no less than 14 competitors from all over Britain.

We adapted to communication with our client by satellite and the entire package was designed, manufactured and co-ordinated with military precision and shipped from the Kent Port of Ridham on time and within 8 weeks of signing the contract.

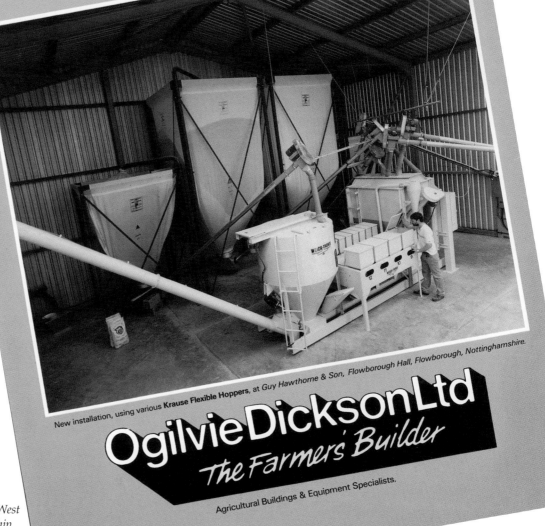
Successfully negotiating with Krause of West Germany for their British Distributorship brought me into contact with a huge range of new customers.

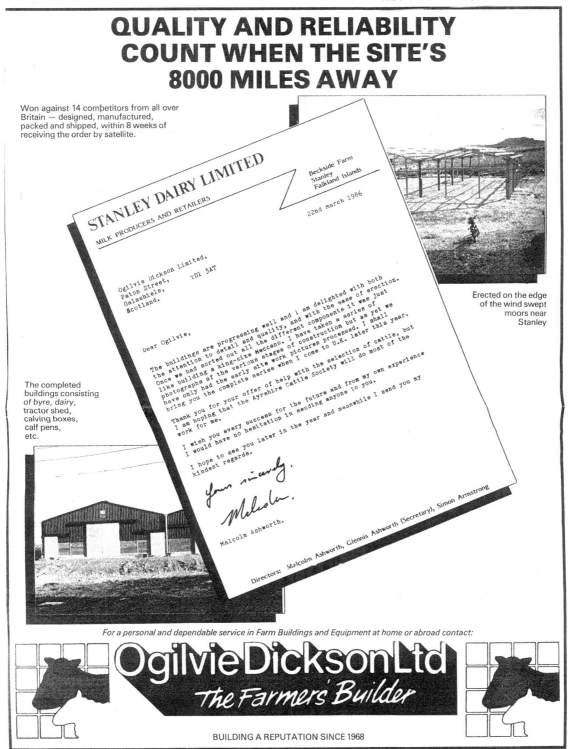

QUALITY AND RELIABILITY COUNT WHEN THE SITE'S 8000 MILES AWAY

Won against 14 competitors from all over Britain — designed, manufactured, packed and shipped, within 8 weeks of receiving the order by satellite.

STANLEY DAIRY LIMITED
MILK PRODUCERS AND RETAILERS

Beckside Farm
Stanley
Falkland Islands

22nd March 1986

Ogilvie Dickson Limited,
Paton Street,   TD1 3AT
Galashiels,
Scotland.

Dear Ogilvie,

The buildings are progressing well and I am delighted with both the attention to detail and quality, and with the ease of erection. Once we had sorted out all the different components it was just like building a king-size Meccano. I have taken a series of photographs of the various stages of construction but as yet we have only had the early site work pictures processed. I shall bring you the complete series when I come to U.K. later this year.

Thank you for your offer of help with the selection of cattle, but I am hoping that the Ayrshire Cattle Society will do most of the work for me.

I wish you every success for the future and from my own experience I would have no hesitation in sending anyone to you.

I hope to see you later in the year and meanwhile I send you my kindest regards.

Yours sincerely,

Malcolm.

Malcolm Ashworth.

Directors: Malcolm Ashworth, Glennis Ashworth (Secretary), Simon Armstrong.

Erected on the edge of the wind swept moors near Stanley

The completed buildings consisting of byre, dairy, tractor shed, calving boxes, calf pens, etc.

For a personal and dependable service in Farm Buildings and Equipment at home or abroad contact:

Ogilvie Dickson Ltd
The Farmers' Builder

BUILDING A REPUTATION SINCE 1968

One of my most successful adverts.

I built a few domestic houses: this one, our home in Galashiels, plus a number which I let as holiday homes.

JOHN RIDGWAY
SCHOOL OF ADVENTURE

Ardmore,
Rhiconich, By Lairg,
Sutherland IV27 4RB.
Scotland
Tel. Kinlochbervie (097 182) 229

Ogilvie Dickson Ltd
85 Queen Street
Galashiels TD1 1QF

3 October 1991

Dear Ogilvie,

Thank you very much for putting up the fine building so
rapidly. We are thrilled with it, and its potential, out
here in such a remote spot. It was fun to see all the
materials coming off the truck so swiftly and onto the barge
for towing across the loch: four and a half hours was a
record for us.

Derek was an excellent ambassador for you, he did a great job
faultlessly, in difficult conditions. We never thought he'd
have the building erected in ten days, but he did, and this
saved us a lot of time with the weather.

Best wishes,

John Ridgway

7.30am 18th September 1991   The
building components being loaded with the
aid of a hydraulic jib onto a small basic sea
going barge.

10.00am — The building now on its way
across the Loch being towed by the Fish
Farm Workboat.

Many interesting contracts were completed, e.g. the new dairy buildings at Beckside Farm near Stanley on the Falkland Islands, a new lobster transit building incorporating sea water tanks on Orkney, a salmon hatchery on Unst and storage buildings on Yell and mainland Shetland, 18 crofter buildings on North Uist, Benbecula and South Uist, including the building of Lochmaddy Auction Mart, a building on Colonsay, four crofter buildings on Tiree, buildings on Coll, Mull and Arran. Other island contracts included a builders' merchant's store, a yacht repair building and many crofter buildings on Skye, buildings on little Cumbrae and the Isle of Bute and 2 quarter-million pound contracts on the Isle of Man.

I therefore amassed considerable experience of building on islands and remote locations, but one of my major building challenges was certainly Ardmore. At this site the nearest road was three miles away and all supplies had to be transported by sea and manually off-loaded!

10.20am — On arrival at Ardmore, manual
offloading takes place quickly to keep the
barge afloat during high tide.

"Up the beaches" with heavy galvanised
girders, rafters, purlins, etc.
12 Noon — We are ready to erect.

A section of the newly opened extension at the Home Improvement Centre in Galashiels, showing the comprehensive range of products now on sale, with the timber-cutting service area in the background.

HOME IMPROVEMENT CENTRE

GALASHIELS LIMITED

Not all businesses go according to plan.

2   The Southern Reporter & Border Standard, December 9, 1976

FIREMEN from Galashiels and Melrose fight to contain the fire at the D.I.Y. Centre in Paton Street, Galashiels, last Friday.

Fire-ravaged centre prepares to re-open

PLANS are already in hand for the rebuilding of the D.I.Y. and Home Improvement Centre in Paton Street, Galashiels, which was ravaged by fire last Friday morning.

Mr Ogilvie Dickson, the owner of the centre, said on Tuesday that he will begin rebuilding as soon as authority can be granted and he hoped to reopen very quickly.

The centre, which had been open for only six weeks, caught fire during the night and firemen were alerted only when the flames burst through the roof at about 7.30 on Friday morning.

The roof of the building was completely destroyed, as were most of the stocks in the centre. Fire tenders from Galashiels and Melrose attended the blaze, which was quickly brought under control.

Fears that the fire would spread to the neighbouring Garden Centre, also owned by Mr Dickson, was alleviated as the firemen contained the fire inside the one building.

The blaze began when several rolls of polythene caught fire from a paraffin heater which had been left on all night.

Mr Dickson said that over £30,000 worth of damage had been done. The heater had an automatic cut-out mechanism in the event of it falling over, but unfortunately the rolls of polythene fell against the heater and caught alight.

Mr Dickson's plant hire equipment was unharmed by the fire, thanks to the speed of the firemen in getting the blaze under control.

Both the plant hire business and the Garden Centre will continue to operate as before. It was revealed yesterday that fire-prevention officers had been called to check the building last Monday but unfortunately they had not appeared.

One of the very first cheques from my company.

My futuristic design and administration office, plus four storage buildings designed and built by my own team.

Introducing the Rt Hon David Steel now Lord Steel of Aikwood at the opening of my new premises.

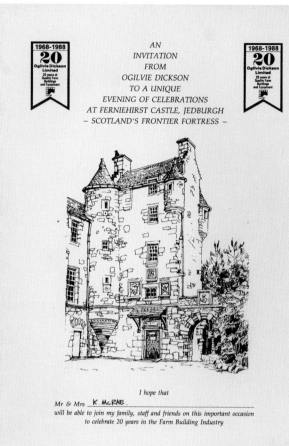

*AN
INVITATION
FROM
OGILVIE DICKSON
TO A UNIQUE
EVENING OF CELEBRATIONS
AT FERNIEHIRST CASTLE, JEDBURGH
– SCOTLAND'S FRONTIER FORTRESS –*

I hope that

Mr & Mrs **K. McRAE**

*will be able to join my family, staff and friends on this important occasion
to celebrate 20 years in the Farm Building Industry*

All work and…

Almost every year I would endeavour to arrange some form of social event and my 20th Anniversary was no exception. Guests were bussed to the spectacular Ferniehurst Castle for an evening's entertainment in extraordinary surroundings. As the night wore on 'Ken the Minstrel' rose to his feet with his back to the dying embers and surprised everyone with a rendering of his poem.

*Family friends since our children's schooldays
Ogilvie   Flora   Ken McRae   Mina his wife*

A TRIBUTE TO OGILVIE.

The auld grey keep at Ferniehirst
　　　For centuries withstood
The reivers and the Border clans
　　　In battles rough and rude.

Kerrs had reigned since lang, lang syne
　　　Through war and peaceful times
And for centuries this gallant clan
　　　Revenged on English crimes.

They rode agin' the Armstrongs
　　　And never were they bate,
Kerrs ruled supreme at Ferniehirst
　　　Till December eighty-eight.

Then, one dark night, a piper played
　　　A lament, 'twas full of grief
For the Dickson clan were in the Hall
　　　Wi' Ogilvie their chief.

How came they there that winter night
　　　That gallant Border clan?
The music ceased, harps were stilled
　　　As the minstrel's tale began . . .

The lovely hills o' Liddesdale
　　　Are a' sae rough and steep
And ower that wild and rough terrain
　　　The Dicksons tended sheep.

Ogilvie, the younger son,
　　　Brought up among these knowes,
Loved to wander in the hills
　　　And coont his faither's yowes.

But Saturdays were special,
　　　He used to take his bike
And, after coontin' a' the sheep,
　　　He'd cycle intae Hawick.

Dancing was his special joy,
　　　He loved to swivel hips,
Military two-steps, palais-glides,
　　　Then off for fish and chips.

But the joys of youth they fade away
　　　And called to arms was he,
Ogilvie answered the Queen's command
　　　And joined the K.O.S.B.

After training days at Berwick
　　　His service took him far
To the jungle in Malaya
　　　Driving the Colonel's car.

After travelling far in foreign lands
　　　He took his last parade,
But no longer felt like coontin' sheep
　　　So he joined the building trade.

He drove a Crawford's JCB
　　　Up hills and over dales,
But building skills were not enough,
　　　By now he fancied sales.

An honest, handsome fellow,
　　　At selling he proved dab,
Clean and tidy, tall and spruce,
　　　He'd also the gift o' the gab!

But he still loved to dance on a Saturday night,
　　　From Hawick to tar off Brora,
Till in the Palais in Glasgow one fateful night
　　　He tangoed into Flora.

This bright young lass frae doon the Clyde
　　　At first felt less than fervant,
Pursued by a Borderer and a salesman at that!
　　　And she was a Civil Servant!

But Ogilvie knew he'd met his fate,
　　　He was a love-sick man,
And his BEST and biggest sale to date
　　　Was when Flora joined his clan.

They settled doon in auld Dumfries,
　　　A toon that's neat and trim,
And Ogilvie did more than sell
　　　- The proof's wee Flo and Jim.

But Ogilvie still was restless,
　　　A man with ambitious dreams,
Farming, building and selling
　　　All figured in his schemes.

His plan was to erect farm buildings
　　　From Tweed to Firth of Lorne,
And in selling, planning and building,
　　　Ogilvie Dickson Ltd. was born.

By now he'd flitted tae Gala,
　　　Flags flew in that wee Border toon
When Ogilvie opened an office
　　　And was off on his trip tae the moon.

The rest of this tale is a legend,
　　　How Ogilvie followed his star
All over the wide Scottish nation
　　　In his BMW car.

Taylors, Elliots and Stewarts,
　　　Silage, silos and sheep,
High-level slatted buildings,
　　　When did he manage to sleep?

West Germany, Australia, the Falklands,
　　　Hoppers, slurry and slime,
I'd love to tell the whole story
　　　But I havenae got enough time.

From a cubicle shed in Annan,
　　　He rose like a rocket to fame,
It's all on the back o' your programme,
　　　Read it when ye get hame.

The Dicksons are great entertainers,
　　　Many parties I fondly recall
At venues all over the Borders,
　　　I've been a guest at them all.

At Peebles, Melrose and Selkirk,
　　　A Bon-Accord spree was the first,
And to cap these events and adventures,
　　　Tonight we're in auld Ferniehirst.

So, a toast to our host and our hostess,
　　　I think we should give them three cheers,
For the friendship, the fun and the mem'ries
　　　Of these TWENTY WONDERFUL YEARS.

Written, with much affection, for our esteemed
friends, Ogilvie and Flora, celebrating the 20th
Anniversary of Ogilvie Dickson Ltd. In Ferniehirst Castle,
Jedburgh, on Friday evening, 9th December, 1988.

Jack Lawson, Director of Livestock Services, Scottish Milk Marketing Board, views his 115' x 130' hot-dip galvanised, insulated building at **Newlands Cattle Breeding Centre** at Scone, Perthshire. **Mr Lawson** states :– "*the ultimate in bull-comfort and ease of management; the entire contract was completed to our total satisfaction, on time and within budget*'.

From a 'hole in the ground' to a whole new Mart in 9 weeks flat!
At **Lochmaddy,** with a very strict timetable and a sale date already set, it was essential that the construction of the Mart was completed on time

the correct Choice !

1968 **25** years 1993

ROBERT WISEMAN & SONS LIMITED
HEAD OFFICE:
159 GLASGOW ROAD, EAST KILBRIDE, GLASGOW G74 4PA
TELEPHONE: 03552 44261   FAX: 03552 30352

Invoice No. 4140
4170

Super job !

WITH COMPLIMENTS

Publicity

The lifeblood of any company is publicity and to publicise a new lightweight aluminium building from Canada, I hired a helicopter from Glasgow Airport to enable me to drop the lightweight components directly on to the site. I had planned to fly it over Glasgow to the site at Helensburgh, but I was not allowed 'just in case the ropes broke'! I invited BBC Television and was able to have 10 minutes free coverage on their agricultural programme! For 26 years I produced all my own advertising and wrote all my own PR items for the press.

Lift off.

Careful manoeuvring on site.

The finished equestrian building.

Glasgow Garden Festival – Gold Medal Winner
One of our most prestigious contracts for our clients: The Edinburgh Woollen Mill, Langholm. The unique nature of the building to house 'The Story of Scottish Wool' earned it a Gold Medal Award.

One of my final building contracts before retirement was this prestigious horticultural store/workshop and gardeners' facilities in Holyrood Park, Edinburgh for Historic Scotland.

Galashiels Garden Centre

My garden centre, one of the first in the Borders, was perhaps one of my favourite businesses, so relaxing and so therapeutic, if only to admire the floral artistry of my Dutch professional florist. I certainly do not regret the diversity of my portfolio, from my freezer centre, one of the first in the Borders, tool-hire and home improvement centre, one of the first in the Borders, Holiday homes with guests from as far afield as Germany and Hong Kong, but after driving 1,151,715 miles in 42 vehicles, I thought it was time to retire.

My most memorable car was undoubtedly my very first privately owned car, the new Hillman Imp. It had a great personality and was a superb car to drive, but oh these water pumps that packed in at the most inconvenient locations.

I had two BMW 3 series which created a record that, had I had it witnessed, would have gone down in Motoring History. Both cars were purchased new and in two consecutive years each car covered 41,927 miles in 11-month periods, driving around my building sites in Scotland, a billion to one chance of a repeat.

– AN OGILVIE DICKSON COMPANY –

CAR MILEAGES – From 1956 onwards

Standard Vanguard Malaya	18,862
Ford 5 cwt. Van Grey	21,500
Ford Anglia Black Levers	4,005
Estate Car Morris Levers	1,000
Morris 1768UG	49,702
Morris MBG559	2,910
Morris MBG631	63,781
Hillman Imp BSM445C	17,056
MLG345C Cortina	63,300
XTU81F Cortina	13,000
NGG622F Cortina	36,656
Cortina Grey	29,000
Cortina Red	27,000
Ford Escort Van	4,000
Ford Cortina Bronze	27,000
Ford Cortina Red	25,000
Transit Van	3,000
Ford GXL White	28,408
Ford GXL Red	25,800
Transit Van	1,000
Ford GT White	28,000
BMW Beige	25,000
BMW Yellow	49,000
Mini Yellow	2,000
BMW Green	36,324
BMW Red	27,835
Renault Yellow	2,000 (approx)
BMW Red	39,215
BMW Silver	41,927
BMW 323i Yellow	107,155
BMW 323i Red	41,927
BMW 325 Silver/Beige	33,300
BMW Charcoal	38,057
Merc Beige (tipped upside-down near Pitlochry)	33,000
Astra (Hire)	3,800
Ford Sierra (Hire)	4,000
302E Merc (On Loan)	700
190E Merc (J) Smoke Silver	43,380
190E 2.0 Merc Beige	43,000
White Van (Accident)	5,462
190E Merc Beige	42,253
190E Merc Beige	42,400

TOTAL VEHICLES = 42 NO.
TOTAL MILEAGE = 1,151,715

FARMERS GUARDIAN, November 14, 1997 13A

Buildings industry has lost its personal pride

THERE is a crying need for greater involvement of architects and designers in the construction and erection of farm buildings, Ogilvie Dickson, a leading Scottish farm builder, told the conference.

He said the farm buildings industry had lost its personal pride, largely as the result of the past widespread availability of grants for farm buildings.

"I was born in 1937 when livestock was housed in superbly constructed, well sited and attractive farm buildings. Sixty years later these same farm buildings are now the preferred accommodation for many human beings.

"Sixty years from now, will humans want to live in our white monstrosities with which we are currently in the process of blotting the rural landscape? I doubt it.

"We have lost our personal pride. In the 1950s when I got ready for dancing I would wear my best Burton or Hepworth suit complete with collar and tie. Now track suits, trainers, jeans, tee shirts are the norm.

"The farm buildings industry has basked in an era of substantial Government aid and farmers should have used this to greater effect. But what happened? To obtain grant the cheapest scheme only was approved, which in many cases means cheap and nasty. This was with absolutely no input from the planning authority other than possibly requiring a blue roof.

"The industry was virtually unregulated as far as aesthetics and design were concerned," said Mr Dickson.

"How can we improve? Farmers are hugely competitive by nature. Why do you think, when so much has changed, farms still support so many agricul-

Ogilvie Dickson

tural shows? Or when a neighbour buys a BMW or a Mercedes, they all want one! It is the competitive spirit. Substantial improvements should therefore be quite easily obtainable by setting an example," he said.

Mr Dickson said that builders, with the help of architects, designers, and planners, should rethink the design of their buildings.

Overhanging eaves with contrasting colours for roof and side cladding should be the norm. Doors should be only in coloured cladding, not garish galvanised sheets, he said.

Intermittent roof lights enhanced geometry and continuous roof strip lighting should be abolished.

Planners should have proper consultancy meetings on site to implement works such as landscaping and tree planting.

The leaving of heaps of excavations on site that would be removed only when the building was extended 10 years later should not be allowed, said Mr Dickson.

"By setting examples of excellence the buyer would quickly respond," he said.

The Scottish Farmer

December 31, 2005 · 35

lifestyle**farmer**

Winter chaos

YESTER**year:** · By Philippa Stephen

FARMERS AND crofters in Shetland were holding back from calling in outside help, this week 10 years ago, despite the Island Council's declaration of a state of emergency, after blizzard conditions over the festive period.

Minutes after assessing the situation by phone with Shetland NFU president, Addie Doull, Scottish NFU leader, John Ross, said the situation was obviously very bad, Mr Doull had said the severe weather would have to continue for a time before helicopters were called in to drop feed to sheep in outlying areas.

"We have, however, registered with the Scottish Office Agriculture Department, that there may be a problem which will necessitate this type of help," said Mr Ross.

Mr Ross said that, fortunately, many Shetland farmers had heeded the weather warnings and had got feed blocks out to sheep.

ULSTER CLYDESDALE enthusiasts, this week, 10 years ago

10 years ago

■ News that the number of confirmed brown rot cases in the Netherlands jumped to 60 after remaining at 46 for more than two month's, brought a sharp reaction from some Scottish growers. It caused more than a dozen of Scotland's major seed potato producers to announce that they were going to revert to the previous quarantine regime.

25 years ago

■ Farm building contractors were talking themselves, and farmers, into a depression and were consequently suffering from lack of business, said Mr Ogilvie Dickson — one of Scotland's leading contractors — at a Farm Buildings Association meeting in Lanarkshire. He said: "Farmers are highly fashionable people. If we talk depression, farmers will not invest. We must show confidence to bring the farmer's business back. With grant applications running at roughly half of the previous years' levels, Mr Dickson, reckoned that the trade would have to adopt new attitudes if it were to survive.

■ According to a survey carried out by the Aberdeen School of Agriculture on the financial position of farms in the North of Scotland, net profit for the 129 farms covered fell by 20% between 1978/79, and 1979/80, and management and investment income by 22%. Total output, on the other hand, rose by 9%, total variable costs by 15% and total fixed costs by 16%. Year-end overdrafts also rose, by 28%, and this, on top of higher interest rates, caused total interest costs to increase by 70% to £34 per hectare.

50 years ago

■ 1955, it was commented, had been a momentous year when looked at in retrospect. Glorious sunshine brought record temperatures throughout the summer, although, perhaps too dry which could have been cause for complaint, leaving farm workers busy carting water week after week. Almost from New Year's Day in 1955, the weather had taken a turn for the better, a godsend against a spell of frost, and grand tilth was also reportedly obtained from spring cultivations. Some turnip crops however suffered beyond repair from droughts, but September and October rain refreshed the farmland, allowing roots to swell and grow, redeeming the year.

■ 1955 was also to be remembered as being the first complete year of freedom from control of fat stock. The first six months of the year, it was said, would remain long in the memories of feeders of cattle and sheep. A period of record prices ensued, and although scales fell heavily against the feeders of heavy sheep, they had had the consolation of knowing no autumn glut, and no glut on prices as a consequence.

100 years ago

■ With the thirteenth volume of the Scottish Farmer complete this week 100 years ago, the circulation of the paper was said to be at its highest recorded. During 1905 the circulation exceeded, by thousands of copies, that of any other agricultural journal ever before published in Scotland. The heartiest of thanks were issued to those who locally supported the newspaper.

When you appear in one's trade magazines 'yesteryear' section, then you know it must be time to retire!

Chapter 5 – Around the World in 151 Days

As I sailed round the world, I met up with all my family in Bangkok, Thailand, then we travelled by train to Penang. Here we are in front of the Shangri La Hotel, Kuala Lumpur, in 1998 on the eve of the Commonwealth Games. On the left is our Chinese driver who drove us all the way from Penang with his trainee Malaysian driver.

The following article was requested by Freighter Travel Review and, as a result of this, some of my pictures formed a display stand for Canadian Pacific at a special exhibition for sea travel in Montreal, Canada.

From Felixstowe to the Far East, from Tonga to Thamesport

AS WE SIT on the *Contship Vision* berthed in Botany Bay container port in Sydney in Australia with yet another two sailing deadlines having come and gone, I feel this is an opportune moment to start to reflect on our adventure around the world so far.

When my wife, Flora, and I arrived on board we were immediately informed that the stevedores were refusing to work as it was raining and the following day they withdrew their labour to attend a mass union meeting leaving truckers with empty or part-loaded trailers scattered around this huge port.

Why containerships? Well, since Lockerbie, I no longer use aeroplanes but try not to allow this to interfere with my love of travelling.

When in 1996 our son, Jim, informed us that he was being posted to Singapore to assist with the extension of their oil refinery, I confidently informed him that I would pay him a visit. I then set about researching alternative transport with driving or rail the only practical contenders: but with bandits in the Khyber Pass and having been warned of inhospitable toilets on the Trans-Siberian railway, the sea looked the only real alternative. I had heard about banana boats but, as they don't sail east, I had to look for other ships and eventually located a

OGILVIE DICKSON, a retired businessman from the Scottish Borders, sailed around the world in 151 days on five German containerships before taking a Canadian vessel homewards. He also travelled overland on a total of 14 trains.

London firm who booked me on the Maersk Colombo to Singapore, rejoining her on the return voyage from Korea. All in all, this was a voyage of 21,000 miles and certainly whetted my appetite for containership travel.

In 1998, when Jim informed us he was being posted to Thailand to extend yet another refinery and our daughter, Flora, along with another student, had won a competition to design the Scottish team costumes for the Commonwealth Games in Kuala Lumpur, we were given a wonderful opportunity to consider a round-the-world trip. Fifteen

firms were contacted with this complicated agenda and Kevin Griffin of the Cruise People in London was able to provide transport on six containerships, which would meet most of our sea travel requirements.

Felixstowe – Hong Kong

On July 15 it was goodbye to my wife at Edinburgh's Waverley Station and I was on my way around the world.

Later, as I struggled with my over-filled cases at Felixstowe station, the train guard shouted to me 'Michael Palin was photographed on that same spot on his return from one of his "world travels."' However, this unknown traveller was about to join the Pusan Senator, which was in the process of taking on a total of 3,500 containers at Felixstowe Docks.

The vessel was built two years before in Korea and is owned by F Laeisz GmbH of Rostock. She had German officers and Kiribati crew.

A life on the ocean wave: Ogilvie Dickson enjoys a moment on deck, but there are clouds ahead. Tuesday 8th December 1998, mid-Atlantic.

Other passengers included a professional musician from a small island off Vancouver and a retired American couple from Mexico. The gentleman had a huge repertoire of occupations including looking after the Mansion House for Ronald and Nancy Reagan.

Shortly after leaving harbour a message was received changing course for Gioia Tauro in Italy to collect 1,000 empty containers.

We then transited the Suez Canal, followed by two days of being tossed around in the Indian Ocean.

After 16 days at sea, Colombo in Sri Lanka looked like being a welcome break for a run ashore. But we found a country at war, with armed soldiers and police at every corner and a feeling of tension everywhere. There is a tendency in the West to forget this war being waged in the north of the island which has cost 50,000 lives, with 600 soldiers killed in one day recently.

The Hilton appeared a safe haven for meals with my fellow passengers during a 10-hour stay. When our taxi driver, booked to return us to our ship, got lost and continued to drive around in circles (he couldn't speak English) and after asking directions of at least eight people, we decided to abandon the taxi and take to our feet. We managed to get on board with just minutes to spare.

Port Klang in Malaysia was our next stop, after which we moved through the Malacca Strait with fire hoses on deck and floodlights ablaze to ward off pirates. It is not easy to believe that pirates still exist but the threat is taken very seriously by seafarers in those few parts of the world where it is still a problem. Just that very day, the Master received a telex informing him of pirates taking over a small ship just off Singapore.

After 23 days at sea, three days in Hong Kong proved a delightful break. I travelled by bus to Canton in China for a day to soak in as much as was possible in such a brief visit and enjoyed the best Cantonese meal ever in one of the finest hotels in Canton. Then it was back to sea.

Hong Kong – Laem Chabang, Thailand

While checking my travel documentation before leaving Hong Kong. I discovered I had not been given the Singapore phone number of the agent for my next vessel, the *Kota Petani*.

With a hurried fax to London, I discovered she had been taken off charter and now I had no ship for Australia. I realised it was no good panicking, better just to get on with the next stage of the journey. Within weeks and a number of faxes and e-mails, the good news came that she was back on charter and, although a few days late, would be ready for us in Singapore.

As I sailed out of Hong Kong on *Maersk Osaka*, I soon discovered the very high standard of maintenance on this DSB-owned containership with German and Filipino officers and Filipino crew. It was quite a novelty, being the first passenger on this particular route. Another first was a young woman apprentice engineer on board.

Weather conditions were ideal and we soon discovered that we would arrive in Laem Chabang too soon for our offloading programme so there was no alternative other than to drift for a number of hours.

The Captain asked me if I would like to take some photographs of the ship. We gathered our equipment, the gang plank was lowered and we were off on the ship's raft (used for painting the hull) on a mill-pond calm sea off Vietnam, to take some unique photographs. The raft was complete with outboard motor, safety gear, etc.

On arrival in Laem Chabang, my son came onboard and I was taken by the ship's local agent all the way to his rented condominium. This is all part of the service one can encounter in freighter travel.

Thailand – Malaysia

During a three week break in Thailand, I was joined by my wife and daughter who flew in from Beijing in China. We then prepared for the next stage of our journey.

We decided that we would travel as a family from Bangkok to Butterworth in Malaysia by train, taking 24 hours on a fascinating journey. On the way we had to move our luggage six times from different carriages, custom posts, etc., with passengers cooking their highly spiced meals with a primus stove on top of the carriage tables and trying to avoid the wildlife on an unfenced, single-track railway.

We were relieved to be met at Butterworth by our Penang Hotels car, complete with cold, damp towels to freshen us up after an arduous journey.

Four days in Penang and we were off by minibus to Kuala Lumpur for the spectacular first night of the Commonwealth Games and an invitation to the Scottish Sports Council dinner party.

Soon, however, the time came for our family to return to work in Thailand and Scotland so my wife and I moved on to Singapore via Kuala Lumpur's magnificent railway station.

Having served with the Gurkhas during the Malayan Emergency in the 1950s, it was a nostalgic journey for me through familiar territory to Singapore where we had two weeks' enforced holiday on Sentosa Island before boarding *Kota Petani* in Singapore.

Singapore – Australia

My wife was joining me on *Kota Petani* for her very first freighter trip so I was keeping my fingers crossed for good weather and calm seas.

We boarded in bright sunshine to be

The author with Peter, the Master of Kota Petani, ready for a party.

welcomed by our German and Filipino officers and Filipino crew and were the only passengers for the 5-day journey which was to take us to Sydney.

But during a prior visit to the Singapore offices of the ship's agents, I casually requested a copy of the ship's itinerary and found we were heading for Freemantle;

this came as a pleasant surprise.

No sooner had we sailed out between Java and Sumatra and into the open sea of the Indian Ocean, a storm erupted and for the next four days our vessel was battling all the way, with Flora lying prostrate in our cabin unable to eat. It wasn't a very good introduction to containerships!

We e-mailed the ship's Freemantle agent and they kindly arranged to book us into a wonderful old 'gold rush' hotel and, on our arrival, they drove us straight to the door.

This unexpected call at Freemantle gave me the opportunity to achieve my ambition of taking one of the great train journeys of the world: from Perth in Western Australia all the way across to Sydney via Adelaide.

It would be 65 hours and 2,800 miles of wonder and amazement, including 300 miles of the longest, completely straight sections of railway in the world, crossing the famous Nullarbor Plain. We listened intently to instructions: should the train stop, do not get off to take photographs as should you be accidently left behind, you would certainly perish in the waterless desert and searing heat.

We arrived in Sydney far too soon at the end of what was a most memorable train journey.

In Sydney there were harbour tours, city tours, Bondi Beach and a detailed inspection of one of the world's finest buildings, the Opera House. Then on to New Zealand . . .

When in Australia you must meet the natives!

You don't try a three-point-turn when you get lost out in the bush in Western Australia, with no signs, no mobile phone signal, no water and no food!

We stopped for water at Broom which has 3 inhabitants

Sydney Harbour

Sydney – Auckland

Our next ship was the *Contship Vision*, almost new and Korean-built with German and Filipino crew. My wife and I were the only passengers.

Contship Vision was carrying only 3,000 tonnes of containers and the ship became the proverbial cork: no sooner had we left Sydney than we were met by the full wrath of the Tasman Sea. Eating became a difficult occupation and on return to our cabin after our first meal, we found our belongings scattered all over the floor.

Sleeping was impossible as we were being tossed around the bed and, at one point, my wife ended up on the floor. We then decided to try and sleep across the bed, which ultimately proved a success.

It was difficult to forget the Tasman Sea but it was also difficult to forget the warmth of the New Zealanders. In our allocated eight days in New Zealand we were travelling for at least seven of them to enable us to reach Dunedin. Apart from one inter-city bus and one ferry, all journeys were by the superb railway system. On looking through the Christchurch telephone directory, I telephoned at random one of the 12 of the Ogilvie clan featured, a Gordon Ogilvie, and within minutes we were collected at our hotel to be taken for a tour of the area. Then it was on to supper

On our way south to Christchurch we called in at the charming town of Kaikoura

and a good dram of malt whisky at his fireside.

In Dunedin one morning, whilst on the pavement photographing our hotel, a young man came up and started a conversation. He was a young lawyer on his way to court, stopping for a chat with a stranger. We found this during our travels all over New Zealand: people from all walks of life taking the time to speak. Sadly we had to leave, with our next stop being America.

New Zealand – America

On a wet Tuesday afternoon in November we sailed out of Auckland Harbour on *Columbus Victoria*, built over 20 years ago and still spick and span. She is owned by Hamburg-Sud, with German, Polish and Kiribati officers and a crew from Kiribati, formerly the Gilbert Islands.

We were the only passengers, but the ship would normally carry a maximum of eight. She had been converted to include a high-quality passenger lounge, dining room and four double cabins fitted out to high specifications.

As we headed north to Tonga and Samoa, it was time for our next surprise: we were not sailing for Long Island, Los Angeles, as stated on our itinerary but for Honolulu in Hawaii, then on to San Francisco. After six days of sailing the Pacific it was time for a break and what better than an 'Equator-crossing' party, complete with a special certificate? This entailed a wonderful four-course meal with the Captain and his wife and senior officers.

About 3,100 miles from Auckland, we were much ahead of schedule for our harbour slot on Honolulu, so we had 10 hours of drifting: a sea well over 16,000 feet being a little too deep to drop an anchor, of course!

We sailed into the Honolulu container terminal 10 days after leaving Auckland and by the time we had been scrutinised by American customs, it was 2130hrs before shore leave was granted. We invited our Kiribati bosun and his wife to join us for a trip to downtown Honolulu. Our ship's agent kindly gave us a lift in his huge Buick and treated us to a guided tour on the way. We were dropped off at Waikiki Beach, where shops are open until 2300hrs.

It is a fascinating place, but not as fascinating as watching the reaction of the bosun's wife: this was her first trip from the South Sea island of Kiribati, where they live in delightful thatched houses which have no walls: there is no electricity and the cooking is done over an open fire by the sea, with water drawn from a well. The motor car has still to arrive on their remote island.

From leaving Auckland, only three ships were sighted during our entire 15-day crossing of the Pacific Ocean. We were all on deck to sail under the Golden Gate Bridge as we entered San Francisco, a welcome sight even though it is painted red oxide and not gold.

After another customs clearance, we were on our way to our delightful hotel in the Fisherman's Wharf area. With only one night scheduled, time-planning was the key, with a city bus tour being our best bet in order to see as much as possible of this beautiful and contrasting city and to examine the substantial reconstruction work carried out since the recent earthquake.

It would have been wrong to leave San Francisco without first having a run on their famous trolley buses, which travel up and down the many steep hills of that city. As one was reaching its stop at the top of the hill, I jumped on as it took off again. My wife was too slow to join me so I jumped off and landed on my back on the highway, watched by a huge crowd of spectators. With blood pouring from my elbow and nursing a damaged hip, I hobbled back to the hotel for a complete change of clothing.

I thought how lucky we in the UK are in having the National Health Service, as San Francisco's medical care is outrageously expensive. It had to be a do-it-yourself job from the extensive medical kit which forms part of my luggage.

After a very co-operative Chinese laundry removed the blood from my clothing, we were ready for an evening's bus-ride across the bay to Oakland to board the Amtrack American double-deck sleeper train through Oregon to Seattle, eventually reaching our very last country of this mammoth trip, Canada.

Arriving by bus from Seattle at Vancouver Central Station at 0010hrs in a strange country, it was wonderful to have my wife's relations collect us in the middle of the night, and to enjoy a superb bed that, for once, did not move.

From then on an athlete's stamina was essential. Collected by a cousin, we were whisked over the mountains to enjoy beautiful scenery, timber mills, factories, wineries and orchards.

Back in Vancouver, my wife left for Scotland by air while I joined *The Canadian*, the famous train that would take me the 2,664 miles across Canada to Ontario in around 72 hours. The track was built over a five year period in the early 19th century. The journey was a classic.

Montreal – Thamesport

There followed three days in Ontario with the inevitable trip to Niagara Falls, courtesy of another cousin, and then a final train journey to Montreal to board my sixth ship, Canadian Pacific's *Canmar Pride*, at the Racine container terminal.

This was the last leg of my voyage and the vessel would take me to Thamesport near London.

I joined exactly on the day stated on my ticket, even though we had lost eight days in Australia.

I was welcomed by Captain Simcox and his Indian crew to their brand new, Korean-built vessel which is ice-strengthened for uninterrupted operation on the St. Lawrence.

And another party: the author, third from right at the back, enjoys an evening with the crew on Maersk Osaka.

As we sailed down the St. Lawrence after a five hour delay due to fog, I dined with the Chief Officer who informed me that we are carrying large sections for the European Airbus, as well as fruit and hundreds of other items in our 2,000 containers.

We soon passed Quebec and were out into the open sea when a weather report informed us of 60 knot winds. Instructions to change course were given to avoid the worst of the weather which involved sailing south of Newfoundland, adding seven hours to our journey. It was snowing heavily, covering the ship with a thick blanket of snow and ice.

I soon discovered that I had a fellow passenger, a professional photographer from Montreal contracted by the shipowner to photograph the ship in storm conditions for the company's annual report. They mine the coal which helps to make the steel that was used by Daewoo to build the ship.

It is said that the best wine should be kept to the last: well, the food and wine on *Canmar Pride* excelled anything on any other ship. It was, in fact, the most outstanding Indian food I have ever tasted: and this is on a commercial ship, not in some swanky restaurant.

It was eight days of very enjoyable sailing on some of the highest seas experienced on my entire voyage, among a very enthusiastic team from as far north as New Delhi to Bombay and Goa in the south. They were all friendly and interested in discussing their families or their considerable seafaring experiences.

At Thamesport, I made my farewells to my new-found friends and headed to my London hotel by taxi and train. The final day of my adventure dawned at 0600hrs with a taxi to King's Cross station to join my 14th train. Then on to Edinburgh, then a taxi, a bus, another taxi to Galashiels 24 hours ahead of schedule which had been arranged over six months before. Fantastic.

Congratulations are due to those men and women who 'go down to the sea in ships': I have indeed been proud and priveleged to have sailed with them.

Chapter 6 – Charity Events and Retirement

Special party helps the Gurkha Trust

A GALASHIELS man celebrated his 60th birthday by giving a very special thank-you to Gurkha soldiers he served with more than 40 years ago.

Ogilvie Dickson, of Wylies Brae, Galashiels, held the first ever Gurkha curry supper and ceilidh in the Corn Exchange, Melrose to help celebrate his birthday and to raise money for the Gurkha Welfare Trust.

Mr Dickson, a founder member of the Friends of the Gurkhas Scotland, invited guests from as far afield as Inverness in the north to London in the south, with one guest flying in specially from Frankfurt.

Guests were welcomed into the Corn Exchange by the pipe music of Lance Corporal Ramprasad Tamang, currently at the piping school at Edinburgh Castle

The authentic Nepalese curry, which was specially prepared by "The Gurkha" restaurant in Morningside, Edinburgh, was a big hit with the guests.

A German television crew from Berlin caused great excitement when they arrived to film the proceedings.

Entertainment for the evening started with Hazel Devlin and Lawrie Grant, who delighted guests with some popular numbers, and the party continued into the "wee sma" hours with stirring music from Fergus Wood and his Kinlochard Ceilidh Band.

After some community singing, the evening was drawn to a close in the most dramatic form with Jim Amos, of Galashiels, playing The Last Post and with Mr Dickson lowering the Gurkha flag and L/Cpl Tamang playing a lament.

Auld Lang Syne complemented a unique evening and the magnificent sum of £3000 was raised for the Gurkha Welfare Trust.

On my 60th Birthday I organised a ceilidh and raised over £3,000 for the Gurkha Welfare Trust, followed by a ceilidh on my 65th Birthday, raising over £5,000 for the Gurkha Welfare Trust. At a garden party at Thirlestane in July 2006 I raised well over £4,000 for the Gurkha Welfare Trust.

During the Jubilee year, I was appointed Borders Convenor for the Commonwealth Veterans' Jubilee Appeal.

The Southern Reporter, Thursday, January 20, 2000

Children's ward nurses in a spin!

WHEELY GOOD. Hospital staff and their young patients joined some of those responsible for last week's presentation at Borders General Hospital of two electrically-powered Mercedes cars. From left, Rebecca Gillie, of Galashiels; Yvonne Bell, from Bells of Coldstream; Flora Dickson; Kyle McAulay, of Galashiels; Ogilvie Dickson; Joan Spence, clinical services manager for women and child health at the BGH; Jane Lumsden, play assistant; Emma Black, play assistant; Dylan Lazzari, of Tweedbank; and Sister Lesley Horsbrugh. ● Picture by ALASTAIR WATSON.

NURSES on the children's ward at Borders General Hospital — christened Noah's Ark — may soon have to be issued with running shoes to catch their young charges after a recent special delivery.

The reason for their possible future exertions was the presentation of two electrically-powered scaled-down versions of Mercedes sports cars, presented to Noah's Ark from the proceeds of the recent Melrose Millennium Ceilidh.

Held in Melrose's Corn Exchange on Hogmanay, the event raised money for both the cars and more than £1,000 for the Friends of the Gurkhas in Scotland charity.

"The festive season is all about children, but to donate money to the children's ward at our Borders General Hospital didn't feel the same as providing something tangible which would bring undoubted happiness," said ceilidh organiser Ogilvie Dickson.

"So I decided to purchase the two Mercedes SLK toy sports cars from Bells of Coldstream, the local Mercedes dealer."

Hawick signwriters Spectrum Signs did the artwork on the cars free of charge, including the number plates BGH 1 and BGH 2.

"Children at the BGH will no longer be required to be wheeled on a trolley to the operating theatre, but will be able to drive in their electric Mercedes sports cars."

Sister Lesley Horsbrugh commented: "The cars are wonderful. The children drive themselves to theatre rather than be wheeled along on a bed.

"It relaxes them and makes a trip to theatre seem more like a bit of an adventure."

The Waverley Hotel in Melrose was bright with tartan when Ogilvie Dickson, who served with the 63rd Gurkha Infantry Brigade during the Malayan Emergency, celebrated his 65th birthday with a 'Grand Charity Ceilidh' which raised over £5,000 for the Gurkha Welfare Trust. Picture shows Billy McGinley enjoying a 'Highland Reel' with Gurkha Piper Rifleman Rambahadur Bura joining in the fun.

Gurkhas have helped to fight our wars and keep our peace for over 180 years. The Gurkha Welfare Trust meets our debt of honour to these loyal soldiers from the hills of Nepal. As a founder member of the Gurkha Welfare Trust (Scottish) Branch, I have been raising money for the trust for the past 11 years.

(L-R) Flora Dickson; Colourful Local; Ogilvie Dickson;
Brigadier Mervyn Lee, G.W.T. Trustee and Chairman of our Scottish Branch;
Sergeant Hebindra Pun, Queen's Gurkha Signals, and Supporter Durga Patchett.

The Gurkha band proudly enter the arena at Braemar Highland Games,
one of our most enjoyable and colourful fund-raising events.

When we retired to Melrose we purchased and converted an old stable, coach house, haybarn and cottage into our own delightful retirement home.

Retirement, well...it didn't quite work out that way.

I was invited to become a member of Melrose Traders' Association and when I suggested we should consider new entrance signs, I was asked to proceed with my concept/origination sketches and arrange for artwork by John Martin, and these were approved by the Traders' Association and the Community Council.

Arrangements were made with Michael Shepherd Architects to produce drawings, funding was arranged by Melrose Traders' Association and the entrance towers were built to an exceptionally high standard by Neil Galloway Builder, Newstead, Melrose.

Ronald Ford, a great friend from Darnick, was very keen that Melrose should have a pipe band, so Ronald and I pressed on and raised £26,000 and I am delighted the band is now fully established.

During 2002 Provost Bunyan asked me to chair a steering group to examine the possibility of Melrose applying for entry to the 'Scotland in Bloom' competition, and within the short space of two years, we had won 'The most improved large village' and 1st prize in 'Scotland's Floral Gateway' competition (large village category).

After designing a range of planters, I found watering a major problem, so Murray Thom, a committee member, and I travelled all the way to Yorkshire to inspect a watering machine that would persuade the committee to purchase 'Rosie' which has proved so popular.

It was also decided that a new raised flower bed be built in St Dunstan's car park and I was asked to proceed with the project. I sourced re-cycled sandstone from Liddesdale and within weeks their local dyker, John Elliot, completed the project in time for planting.

Melrose

The new raised flowerbed taking shape with dyker John Elliot on the right, from Liddesdale.

An attractive feature for 'Melrose in Bloom'.

Melrose & District Pipes and Drums on their way to the very first Abbey Carol Service.

Inside Melrose Abbey at the very first Abbey Carol Service.

After discussions over coffee my great friend Ronald Ford of Darnick and I were of the opinion that a Melrose Christmas Carol Service should be held in the Abbey and I am proud that Ronald and I were part of the committee who organised the very first Melrose Abbey Carol Service, which is now proving such a hugely popular annual event.

I wonder how many of us are aware of our sayings? Well, on the day I retired I received a number of mine made up in a cheque book from three of my design office staff!

For Pete's sake

It's uncanny

Take a note

Do it yourself, Dickson

It must be telepathy

He Said It ....

It's all about market research

Holidays – holidays should be banned

$1 \ldots 2 \ldots 3. A \ldots B \ldots C.$ (when I was angry)

He's my best customer

Let's have a decka

Re . . ally

Sure as a cat's a beast Eat, Sleep, Dream

I don't want caught with my pants down!

Catch!

It would drive you to drink

That was some marathon.

I'll eat my hat *What a bloke!*

That man, wears me out.

I want a pukka copy

No wonder I have no hair.

Just what I was thinking myself.

I want it in LARGE TYPE.

Double Space **If in doubt – ASK.**

Hope I am not disturbing your steak?

(when I phoned a customer at mealtime)

WELL - What More Can We Say . . . Jane . Paul . Jess.

Book success

OGILVIE Dickson reports that of the 1500 copies of his reference book "Melrose and its People" only 32 remain available for sale.

Those wanting to buy one should telephone Mr Dickson on (01896) 820038 at once to avoid disappointment.

All profits after expenses will go to local charities and in particular to Melrose in Bloom.

Local interest in the book was immense.

Local worthy Angus Mackay finds his own picture in the book.

Melrose
and its People 2002

Edited, Compiled and Published by
Ogilvie Dickson

The Book that all Melrosians have been waiting for!
A HARDBACK IN FULL COLOUR

Never before has such an extensive and historical photographic record been attempted here in Melrose.

For the Jubilee year, I considered it important to record for posterity a photographic record of Melrose, its people, its traders and children. This was produced in hardback and became a Best Seller in the town and surrounding area, selling 1,100 copies in five weeks and the profit of £1,200 was presented to Melrose in Bloom.

*The first copies come off the press
at Buccleuch Printers in Hawick supervised by Scott Emond.*

'More groups, businesses and organisations than I ever imagined exist in Melrose and the immediate surrounding area' says Provost George Bunyan.

 SCOTTISH EXECUTIVE

Home Composting
Ogilvie Dickson

named a 2005
Scottish Borders
Composting Crusader

Helping get garden
waste sorted.

Scottish
Borders
COUNCIL

Reduce Reuse Recycle
let's get it sorted
www.scotborders.gov.uk/recycling

Waste Aware
Scottish Borders

Having been reared in a recycling environment it came as second nature to compost all my garden waste from my organic garden. During my tenure in 'Melrose in Bloom' I delivered and introduced composters to almost 200 householders in the town. I was therefore naturally delighted to become a Composting Crusader.

A Border Ambassador
In the past I have sold our beautiful Borderland to potential visitors from all over the world. In fact, I have often been asked if I work for the local tourist board! I was therefore thrilled to be invited to become a member of our Scottish Borders Ambassadors' Club.

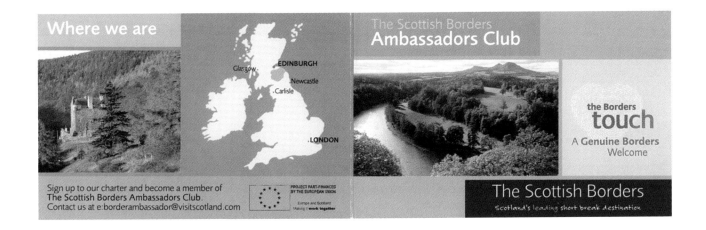

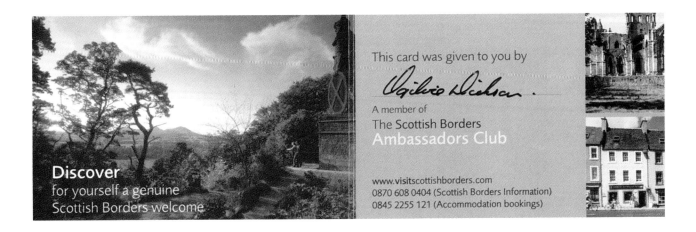

Hobbies in Retirement

My new B.M.W. 1200cc Cruiser renews my youth!

I just couldn't resist it – sitting in the showroom at the dealer where my B.M.W. was being serviced, my '100th Anniversary' Harley Davidson 1200cc Sportster.

Retirement means different things to different people.

To me it means communication. Some time ago, I formed our Tuesday Club so that we could meet every 3rd Tuesday and make educational visits to such places as breweries, distilleries, ancient buildings and it has been known that we even visit certain parliament buildings!

Here we are celebrating a member's birthday.

The Tuesday Club
For Leisure, pleasure and adventure

L-R Wing Commander David Jones; Self; Ronald Kennedy (Jet Pilot) and Managing Director of an international company; Murray Thom, Dentist; Donald McGregor, Bank Manager; Ronald Ford, Company Director, Cashmere.

Photograph Ogilvie Dickson 2005.

Event Organiser Ogilvie Dickson, St John's Cottage, Huntly Avenue, Melrose TD6 9SD
01896-82-0038 ogilvie@dickson5401freeserve.co.uk

Sea Travel

Containership Travel to the Orient.   *Luxury Travel to the South Atlantic.*

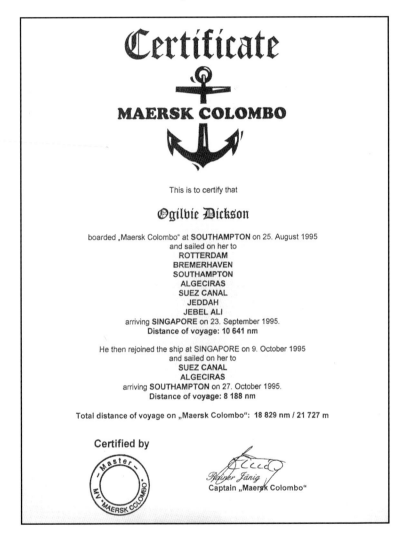

Above is a certificate presented to me at the end of my very first voyage on this rather unconventional form of transport. I was on my way to Indonesia to visit our son Jim and found this East German ship with a Kiribati crew. This was a new experience which encouraged me to consider this form of transport for future leisurely international travel.

I thought the age of technology would pass me by, but 30 days of professional on-board computer tuition provided the necessary stimulus for me to purchase my very first computer.

Considering my connections with Singapore, I am justifiably proud to have some of my pictures, taken during 1956-1958, accepted by Singapore National Museum.

NATIONAL HERITAGE BOARD

*Singapore
History
Museum*

23 July 1996

Mr. Ogilvie Dickson
"Cortachy House"
Wylies Brae
Galashiels
Borders
Scotland

Dear Mr. Dickson,

1. Thank you for your generous donation of photographs as well as your loan of 22 slides.

2. The photographs and slides are useful records documenting the landscape of Singapore in the 1950s, and will be accessioned into our Singapore History Museum permanent collection.

3. We will return the 22 slides as soon as we have made prints of it.

4. Enclosed herewith is our official receipt no. 0214 and two copies of our Deed of Gift for your reference.

5. Please sign one copy of the Deed of Gift and return it to us. The other copy is for your personal records.

6. Thank you very much.

Then...

Yours sincerely,

LIM HOW SENG
DIRECTOR
SINGAPORE HISTORY MUSEUM

93 Stamford Road, Singapore 178897, Republic of Singapore.

...and now!

Chapter 7 – Peebles KOSB Malayan Veterans' Dinner

1689 - 2005

**50th Anniversary of the King's Own Scottish Borderers Malayan Veterans' All Ranks Dinner
in memory of the late Josh White and our other comrades.**

Peebles Hydro Hotel 15th September 2005

Enclosed you will find a unique invitation for you and your wife, or partner, to be part of a very special occasion. We are celebrating the 50th anniversary of the tour that the Battalion, the Kings Own Scottish Borderers spent in Malaya during the counter insurgency operations against the communist terrorists from 1955 to 1958.

We have chosen to hold the reunion at this time because this may possibly be the last opportunity for us to celebrate the event as the King's Own Scottish Borderers in our own right, due to the threat of amalgamation. It is therefore going to be a very special occasion and one which we hope you will wish to take part in for the sake of posterity.

We will have an initial welcoming reception followed by dinner and some good, but short, speeches so that there will be plenty of time to meet our old friends and comrades to talk over old times and remember our Service together.

It is an evening to share not only with our comrades but with our wives and partners so do make it a real 'family occasion'. To allow us to enjoy ourselves, we will have special rates to stay at the Peebles Hydro with other options of inexpensive accommodation – so come along and be prepared to have a really cracking evening!

See you all there!

Full details and a booking form are attached.

Ogilvie Dickson

Peebles Picture Gallery

Some of the proud KOSB soldiers who attended the reunion to the three-year fight against communist insurgents in Malaya.

Grand Draw for the Gurkha Welfare Trust.
I am holding the winning tickets to Malaysia, won by Mr & Mrs Jimmy Roberts, Dalbeattie, with John Cushion, Sales Manager, Malaysian Airlines.

Event organiser Ogilvie Dickson (right) of Melrose, with (from left) Brigadiers Allan Alstead, Frank Coutts and Ian Christie, and KOSB regimental secretary Lt Col Colin Hogg.

The 315 who sat down for dinner.

*Many artefacts were used
to decorate the Hall.*

*Joan White with Drew Scott, Melrose,
who scooped a copy of 'Malayan
Memories' in the draw.*

Thoughts in a Base Camp
written in Yong Peng Camp in Malaya, 1956

O' to be back in Selarang,
To run around with the same old gang,
From the NAAFI shop to Honest Johns,
An easy life from dusk till dawn.

A Saturday night in Singapore,
Around the bars from door to door,
Across the way to the Union Jack,
To where you need no ration pack.

But now we're back in the Federation,
The dam'nest place in all creation,
But on we go no hesitation,
Thro' mud and tropical vegetation.

Thro' rubber jungle steaming swamp,
The land where snakes and lizards romp,
But on we go with no words spoken,
And settle down with backs half broken.

But there'll come a day when it's all over,
And we'll be once again on clover,
Whether by loch or blue lagoon,
I'll never forget old seven platoon.

Viv Sharp, vocalist, poet and one of Hawick's great worthies.

Chapter 8 – Inspired – Encouraged – Influenced

The following chapter is devoted entirely to people who have inspired or influenced me. They are from an extremely wide cross section and are therefore impressively interesting. I have placed them in alphabetical order commencing with someone who, I am in no doubt, inspired me to start my own construction business.

J. S. Crawford

When I joined J.S. Crawford (Builders), like so many who had left National Service with no trade or qualifications, I accepted it as a transient post until such times as my compass would point me in that un-predetermined direction.

I expected to find a builder who would be dressed in overalls and that I would be treated with relatively little respect. How wrong I was! From my very first meeting and throughout my time working with J.S. (Jim) Crawford, I found him a perfect gentleman. He was always immaculately dressed and never did he raise his voice once, but guided and encouraged me and brought out the very best in his fellow men and, at the same time, instilling a great deal of enthusiasm for the construction industry.

James Smith Crawford

James Smith Crawford was born in Melrose in 1909, son of John Crawford (Jock), a baker and trainer with Melrose Rugby Football Club, who had a family of four sons and one daughter.

Jim served his apprenticeship as a stonemason with the local firm of William Spiers. He worked on some very interesting contracts, the Melrose Rugby Football Club stand, which was opened in 1926, the main gates and lodge houses of Floors Castle, and the prestigious Scotsman office in Edinburgh.

He was a noted rugby player, playing for Melrose 1st XV and the South of Scotland. He took part in the famous game at The Greenyards when the South of Scotland drew with the South African Springboks team of the 1933/32 tour in a no-scoring draw.

At the outbreak of war, he worked for two years helping to build ammunitions depots at Charlesfield in St. Boswells, eventually being called up for services with REME in 1941 until his demob in 1945.

It was then that he formed his own construction company which has grown to be one of the leading construction companies in the Borders.

It is interesting to note that one of his first contracts was building the Melrose Rugby Football turnstiles. Other contracts included renovating the George and Abbotsford Hotel for the Vaux Co., Hetties futuristic hair salon, plus a number of housing developments, schools and factories throughout the Borders.

Jim was most ably supported in his business by his wife Annie, who was in charge of the office.

*Brigadier Frank Coutts at the KOSB Malayan Veterans'
50th Anniversary Dinner in Peebles Hydro
15th September 2005*

Brigadier Frank Coutts CBE

What a man... what a career...

Our Borderers' Hero, one of the most inspirational leaders of our time, respected by his soldiers, irrespective of rank or position.

The son of Dr Jack Coutts, Minister of the Church of Scotland in Coldstream, Rangoon, Aberdeen, Glasgow, Milngavie and Melrose.

He embarked on a career with the Metropolitan Police, which was interrupted by war. He then joined the King's Own Scottish Borderers as a Platoon Commander, serving in some of the fiercest battles of World War II.

In the 50's he served in the jungles of Malaya, followed by service in Berlin, and then was appointed a highly popular Colonel of our regiment.

He was known throughout the rugby world, both as an international player and as President of the SRU.

I am proud to have served with him for 11 years in the Gurkha Welfare Trust (Scottish Branch).

At 88, Brigadier Frank is still working for charity and riding his new Honda scooter to and from his allotment, where his love for gardening is still part of his unbelievably busy lifestyle.

I have driven Brigadiers in various vehicles, but never on a mule? A Kawasaki Mule!

Having a tour of Melrose after Brigadier Frank had been presenting the 'Melrose in Bloom' awards the previous evening. (The new watering vehicle is affectionately known as 'Rosie'.)

Margaret Eliott

Chieftain of the Clan Elliot

A return visit to Liddesdale is always looked forward to with great anticipation and to expose Liddesdale to my Tuesday Club for the very first time required some careful planning.

Margaret Eliott, Chieftain of the Elliot Clan and I,
under the Clan Crest at Redheugh, Liddesdale.
There are various spellings of families within the clan.

Hermitage Castle, the Liddesdale Heritage Centre in Newcastleton, are both outstanding locations steeped in history. The heritage centre with a unique collection would prove a hit, but I had a member, an informed historian with an Elliot mother! I couldn't therefore miss the opportunity of a visit to the seat of that legendary Liddesdale Clan, the Elliots at Redheugh.

I thought a visit to the Elliot Museum would fit the bill, but on arrival we were warmly welcomed by the Clan Chief, Margaret Eliott, and ushered into Redheugh for afternoon tea: true Liddesdale hospitality with an enjoyable and informative visit to the museum thereafter.

Rev. Dudley Fox

All in a lifetime

The cover tells it all!

It was during the planning of a Gurkha fund-raising event that Dudley first made contact with me, requesting my assistance regarding the sourcing of a publisher for his book. I just couldn't track one down, so when I made contact again, I suggested that I publish it for him, which was a totally new experience!

From cover design to printing and marketing it was indeed a challenge, but oh, the pleasure!

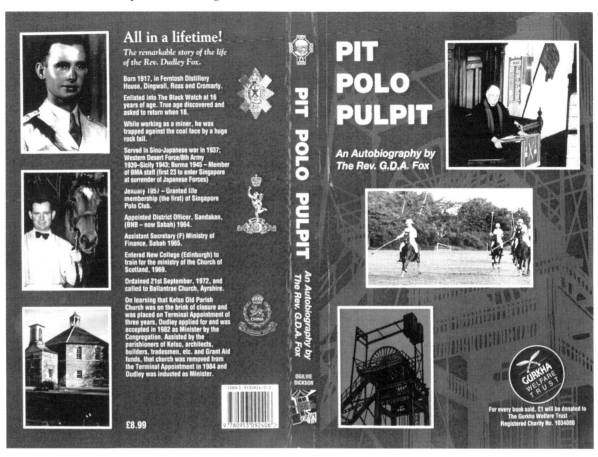

Here we have the book launch and signing outside Kelso Old Parish Church.
Mrs Fox is the third lady from the right with Dudley at his desk.

77

Sir Rex Hunt CMG

Since my youth I have always had an interest in the remote Falkland Islands. I suppose it stemmed from my knowledge of so many Scottish shepherds leaving to establish a new life in the South Atlantic and who now form such robust cornerstones of that isolated community.

Sir Rex and I in discussion.

During the war, I tried never to miss a news bulletin. After having supplied the new dairy buildings to Beckside Farm, Stanley, I decided to sail down on the only ship that I could find heading in that direction.

After dinner one night, as we were sailing off Uruguay, I was up on deck viewing another ship well out to sea, along with only one other person. As is common at sea, we soon entered into conversation and I immediately discovered I was in conversation with my Falkland hero, Sir Rex Hunt, a courageous man who was able to hold the community of the Falklands together under impossible conditions.

To Ogilvie Dickson,
With best wishes,

MY
FALKLAND
DAYS

Rex Hunt

QE2   3/11/03

We stepped downstairs to the lounge for a beer, then real living history unfolded... His radio message to his people 'This is the Governor speaking, this is just to let you know that the first Argentinian ships have been sighted... A few minutes before six o'clock, we heard the sound of gunfire...'

'Sporadic firing from the Argentinians surrounding Government House…'

Three hours later and one of my most enjoyable, exciting and informative interviews ended.

What better place to receive Sir Rex's book, than sailing in the South Atlantic.

Hobkirk Parish Church

Tuesday 12th November 2002

Patrick Anderson Laing, M.C. (Pat)

died 6th November 2002 aged 84 years

Pat Laing MC

To be asked by a family to deliver a Eulogy is difficult, but I thought it my duty, considering that I had known Pat for many years and that he was also a member of my regiment, The King's Own Scottish Borderers. I hope it conveyed his quite unique personality and that we had lost one of the great worthies of our Borderland.

Tribute by Ogilvie Dickson
Friends, we are gathered here today to give thanks for the life of Pat Laing. A modest gentleman who enjoyed the company of Dukes and Duchesses and herd laddies. I know, I was a herd laddie. He became a household name in his own lifetime, here in our Borderland.

'Pat Laing O' Bonchester'
My first recollection of Pat was in my schooldays, when his smoky tractor and stoory, dusty Garvie thrashing mill travelled the farms in my homeland of Liddesdale.

Pat was born at Cleuchhead, Bonchester, on the 11th May 1918, the elder son of Norman and Sarah Laing. He always expected to farm Cleuchhead, but his plans were abruptly interrupted by the onslaught of war and as a T.A. Member, he was immediately called up for service, with our regiment The King's Own Scottish Borderers. During a short training stint in Ireland, Lt Pat found himself billeted in the Bushmill Whisky distillery and with the help of his comrades, was quickly able to liberate the cellars below! It was typical of many of Pat's escapades.

Lt Pat was soon seconded to the Reconnaissance Corps on active service all over Northern Europe on and behind enemy lines. Due to Pat's modest disposition, it was only last week that I discovered that he had been honoured with the Military Cross. I shall read you a small section of the Citation.

At the end of October 1944, when the regiment was holding the Northern part of the Nijmegen Bridgehead at Driel, he with another officer, in five nights, recovered 20 vehicles and equipment, including anti-tank guns and a white scout car which had been left by previous units as being beyond recovery. These jobs were done mainly within 500 yards of the enemy, often under shell and mortar fire, and small arms fire. His officer's resourcefulness, power of leadership and calculated bravery have always produced the highest results from his troops, his unremitting work and cheerful personality have been of incalculable value to his regiment.

Eventually in 1945, Pat was given the horrendous task of liberating a concentration camp.

On demobilisation he enjoyed a brief spell of rural life in the Borders to be changed by the loss of his father. He then embarked on a new venture, farm contracting, which was to lead him to his first grey lorry, part of his lime-spreading enterprise, and here again, I came in contact with Pat's lorries hauling for my then employer Millicans.

On the 15th June 1956 Pat managed to take a day off work to marry Shirley, his wonderful wife of 46 years.

Pat's contracting business soon expanded into bracken crushing, mole draining, baling, ploughing etc and by the 1960's Pat was developing his haulage business with his famous grey lorries, to be seen from Lairg to Land's End.

His business continued to develop with the assistance of his very loyal staff, leaving him more time to concentrate on his love of horse and livestock haulage. Generally, a typical week was local markets, Tyneside on a Friday, driving customers to the hounds, point-to-point, Border Common Ridings, shows and pony club events at weekends.

Pat never had time for holidays and he never wore a watch.

Pat's business became even more varied, hauling my farm buildings all over Scotland including the Hebrides, Pringles Sweaters, corned beef from the docks to Glasgow, ponies to Wembley, whale carcasses from the shore at North Berwick, and sheep for evermore. He had the amazing knack of dealing with such a variety of customers.

Pat's office system, oh my, it was unique. It consisted of the top pocket of his bib and brace overalls, which contained... messages for next week's work, names and addresses, numbers of loads, directions, receipts, bills with cash and all details on the back of his Capstan full strength cigarette packet and, on running out of space, Pat would just smoke all the more!

With a combination of barley anns, threshing dust, slag and Capstan full strength, an investigation was arranged at Peel hospital and, at that point, son Hugh came home from Edinburgh to help and only when leaving hospital were Capstans discarded for sweets.

Pat never gave up his love of driving and even at the age of 80, he could be seen all over the Borders in his beloved Mercedes on what he termed 'local deliveries' consisting of any point North of Newcastle to the Scottish Highlands.

When asked about retirement, his reply 'Neither the bank manger nor the wife will allow me!'

We are going to miss Pat, his cheerful smile, his quick sense of humour, his enormous repertoire of reminiscences.

'Pat O' Bonchester'

**It has indeed, been a privilege
to be your friend.**

Pat when he was transferred to Reconnaissance.

Pat in his natural surroundings.

Inside Abbotsford House, 27th July 2002.

Dame Jean Maxwell-Scott.

At the time of producing my book 'Melrose and its People', I called on Dame Jean to discuss the possibilities of having pictures taken within that Scottish architectural treasure, Abbotsford House.

I was met with warmth, charm and courtesy by that very graceful lady, Dame Jean, who gave me total freedom to complete my photographic shoot within Abbotsford.

My favourite picture is that of Dame Jean Maxwell-Scott, direct descendant of Sir Walter Scott, and I in front of the most famous painting in Abbotsford, that of Sir Walter Scott and Robert Burns at their only meeting, at the house of Professor Adam Ferguson, in the Sciennes District of Edinburgh, when Scott was just 15.

Abbotsford House.

From Kazan on the Volga 420 miles North East of Moscow.

Reseda Muir, Perth

It was a phone call from the North of Scotland College of Agriculture, asking if I would sponsor a young Russian architect on a visit to Scotland, that gave me my very first introduction to Reseda.

I welcomed her to the Borders with a 12 hour whistle-stop tour, which commenced with coffee at our home, a Model T Ford Rally, a Border Food Exhibition, a visit to one of our Mill Shops, an interview on Border Television, then dinner at a local restaurant.

After that I said goodbye as she was leaving the next day by Aeroflot, on a flight back to Russia.

I expected that I would never see her again; fortunately that was not to be the case, as that charming, talented lady has now become a great friend of our family.

I could never forget Reseda, sitting round our kitchen table telling us all about her life in Russia as a child. I asked her if she would give her story to me in the written word: well here it is and I am sure you will find it fascinating...

Kazan

I was born in Kazan, on the Volga, 420 miles North East of Moscow. Kazan is a modern city with a population of 1.8 million. In the Middle Ages it was the capital of Kazan Khanate, one of many independent Muslim states in Central Europe.

In 1551 Queen Suumbike was deposed by Tsar Ivan IV ('The Terrible') whose Russian nation devoured and Christianised the old Khante of Kazan, sweeping down to the Caspian in later years.

Kazan jewellers made the so-called 'Kazan hat' taken to Moscow and used to crown the Russian Tsars thereafter.

Links with the East remained. My great-grandfather (my mother's grandfather) was a businessman who traded Turkish carpets and spices. Everything changed in the 1917 Communist Revolution. Kazan became heavily industrialised with everything under state control. When I was little, I wore a red scarf and a badge with Lenin's face on it. Later I trained as an Architect in one of Kazan's Universities.

Granny's Village

As a city girl I loved visiting my Grandmother's village in the country, where the old rural domestic lifestyle survived. The village was made up of small wooden houses and was eight hours away by train. We had to wave and shout for the ferryman to row across the river to collect us.

One of my Aunts was a beekeeper on a collective farm. I was allowed to dress up in her protective clothing and watch honeycombs being collected. Alongside the state collective farms every household had their own animals and vegetable garden. My favourite animal was my Aunt's black bull, called Mishka.

There were wild animals too, in the surrounding forest. As a boy, my father was once chased by a pack of wolves in deep winter and once when out for a walk, I narrowly escaped being trampled by a moose. My Granny, like other women in the village, made long rugs from recycled pieces of cloth.

My Grandfather (my father's father) was the Collective Farm's chairman. He was killed in the Second World War. His family survived because they had a large garden and their cow's milk.

Electricity came to the village as a result of a new hydroelectric dam built in the 1970's but as a result of the dam, many villages were flooded as was half of my Grandmother's garden. Also as the water became still, it became coloured with beautiful white and yellow water lilies.

Volgograd

When I was 14, my mother and I went on a three-week cruise on the Volga. Starting in Kazan, we travelled up river by canal to St. Petersburg before returning back past Kazan all the way down to the southern end of the Volga where it meets the Caspian Sea at Astrakhan.

Each day the ship would stop at a new place, town or city for the passengers to explore. As a teenager, I was unmoved by all these beautiful historical towns and cities, but now I realise they made a lasting impression.

This single biggest impact at that time, came from the giant statue of 'Mother Russia'. It is 50% larger than the Statue of Liberty in New York and is a memorial to the one million people who died in the Second World War battle of Stalingrad.

Astrakhan at the southernmost point of the journey was formerly capital of Astrakhan Khanate. It is famous for the caviar of the Caspian Sturgeon.

Sviyazhsk

Sviyazhsk was built in 1551 by the Tsar Ivan IV ('The Terrible') as a stronghold. From there he attacked for the third time and finally conquered Kazan in 1552. Prefabricated buildings were made in Ooglich near Moscow and floated down the Volga to Sviyazhsk, where a fortress was created in three weeks.

During my architectural study at University, I was a member of an extra-curricular group studying historic architecture. In summer we stayed in monks' dormitories on a beautiful island of Sviyazhsk on the Volga. Using old methods, we restored a 17th Century 'trapeznaya' part of an old church, where the monks had their meals and gatherings.

At that time, there was a psychiatric hospital in one of the monasteries and we could see outside patients with shaven heads wearing long robes.

There were four monasteries on this small island with 16 – 17 century frescoes still remaining. One of the frescoes shows St. Christopher with an unusual head. The local tradition is that he was given an animal head by God in response to his prayer, asking not to be so handsome because he was a serious preacher!

Nizhnii Novgorod

Nizhnii Novgorod is three hours' fast hydrofoil journey up river from Kazan. After graduating from university, I was sent there to work for an atomic power design institute as an architect. My job was to design houses for power station workers.

During this period of my life it was very exciting to live in Russia. Perestroika meant that new ideas were openly being discussed and private enterprise encouraged, new freedoms were being explored and democracy was being introduced. It was a new Dawn for the country and also for me. In my spare time I worked for an underground newspaper, an icon studio and participated in some TV programmes. I watched a TV programme on the communist coup day. The presenter said 'we should resist... you may see me for the last time...'

I left the institute and worked for the first private architectural practice to be established in the city. This enable me to move into my first rented flat, in one of the thousands of faceless high-rise blocks on the edge of the city.

'Big Volga' Design Seminar

The Volga formed the backdrop for an international design seminar held in 1991. Architects from Scotland, Italy, Germany and Russia came together for one week on board a ship. The purpose of the seminar was to tackle the problem of where to relocate thousands of people as part of a major modernisation and restoration of the old city centre of Kazan. For me as a young architect, this was not an abstract academic exercise but a chance to see how fellow professionals addressed similar problems in real life.

The ship would stop at many towns on the river and participants had the opportunity to discover and explore the historic towns and their buildings. These would then be used in our discussions.

As well as being an intellectual journey and an opportunity to exchange ideas, the trip was also highly sociable and fun and laid the foundation of good friendships.

River Kerzhenets

In 1997 I went on a canoe trip with friends on the River Kerzhenets, a tributary of the Volga near Nizhnii Novgorod. We arrived at our departure point by bus and assembled our aluminium framed canoes out of big bags we carried from the city. We spent a week travelling by boat down river surrounded by wild forests.

On our journey we would occasionally come upon small timber villages, which had no road access and had been bypassed by the modern world. The villages would always have a number of wells for water and many of the houses were empty. Old ladies sitting on their benches on the front of their houses would implore us to stay as all young people had left to go to the cities.

We came across a fisherman who used a dug-out canoe. He fished with a net that he would string across the river and a long stick, which he would plunge into the water to scare the fish. He had a beautiful collection of small fish in his basket.

Overnight we would camp on the riverbank and would sing songs and tell stories around the campfire while our porridge boiled.

The downside of the trip were the clouds of the enormous hungry mosquitoes, which would descend upon us as soon as we set foot on land.

At the end of the journey we arrived at Markariev Monastery, a medieval complex that had closed during the Soviet era, but had newly reopened at the time.

St. Petersburg

Connected by canals to the Volga River, St. Petersburg is located at the eastern end of the Baltic Sea. Founded in the 17th century by Peter the Great as Russia's window on the West and as a bastion against Swedish expansion, the city was constructed on a number of islands by piling into marshy ground. The wooden foundation piles currently suffer the same problems as they do in Venice; increased water table fluctuations.

My first impression of St. Petersburg as a student was how light and beautiful it was with its opening bridges and wonderful opera. I loved reading its writers and poets such as Alexander Pushkin, Fyodor Dostoevskii and Anna Akhmatova.

Only after moving to Scotland in 1994, did I become aware of the links between the two countries. Charles Cameron and other Scottish architects, town planners and masons, as well as military servicemen, served Catherine the Great. Much of the city's 18th century wrought iron work was produced in Scotland.

One of my assignments in Scotland was with a firm who worked on the redevelopment of the building in the centre of St Petersburg where Dostoevsky lived and wrote his novel 'White Nights'.

All paintings by Reseda Muir.

Items Reseda doesn't mention is that she lectured at Elmwood College, Cupar, Fife on landscape design and graphic presentation, qualified LLM in Glasgow, and is now in partnership with her husband in their highly successful architectural practice in Perth. It was they who designed the conversion work of our new home in Melrose.

Reseda's story formed part of a joint exhibition with Robin Bell, Scottish writer, illustrator and poet. The exhibition 'My River, Your River' (The Volga and The Tay) was held during 2006 in the Ferguson Gallery, Perth.

Reseda in our garden on her very first visit to Scotland.

Here I am giving away Reseda at her wedding to her handsome Scottish architect husband, Ian Muir of Perth, on the right of the picture at the Balmerino Manse near Wormit, Fife.

Tom Russell OBE CBE CMG
Gattonside, Melrose

Tom Russell is an outstandingly interesting man educated at Hawick, St Andrews and Cambridge, serving in the 2nd World War, initially in the Black Watch, eventually commissioned to the Cameronians and finally transferred to the Parachute Regiment.

Tom experienced a ferocious battle and was, for 15 months, a prisoner of war. I still re-read that awful moment in his book 'As the fire fight was intensifying and grenades were exploding, a machine gun bullet struck me at the top of the left thigh. I passed out from pain and loss of blood. Two parachutists appeared to help me, with my broken leg bouncing down the stairs…'

In captivity there was a washing area in the middle of the room, with one tap for 130 men. This was off at certain times of the day!

After War Service he joined the Colonial Administrative Service, eventually promoted Chief Secretary of the Western Pacific High Commission, and in 1974 he was appointed Governor of the Cayman Islands.

Flora and I with Tom Russell OBE CBE CMG, attending one of Brigadier Frank Coutts CBE's famous Gurkha Curry Lunches at Redford Barracks, Edinburgh.

Baroness Thatcher

Over the years I have had the privilege of interviewing people from all walks of life, but I have got to say that to have the opportunity to interview Margaret Thatcher, one of the greatest Prime Ministers of the 20th Century, was a unique experience, one which I will never forget!

THE FALKLAND ISLANDS GOVERNMENT RECEPTION

.... Mr. Ogilvie Dickson ....

IS INVITED
TO A RECEPTION ON WEDNESDAY 8th JUNE 2005
AT 6.30 PM
IN **THE GREAT HALL**
LINCOLN'S INN, LONDON WC2

. THE BAND OF THE IRISH GUARDS WILL BEAT RETREAT

025   PLEASE BRING THIS INVITATION WITH YOU AS IT ACTS AS A SECURITY CHECK

She may not have agreed with my suggestion of a new leader, but I found her exceedingly polite. Baroness Thatcher – 8th June 2005.

Chapter 9 – KOSB Malayan Veterans' 2006 trip to Malaysia

King's Own Scottish Borderers
Malaya 1955 - 1958

Malaysia 2006

PROPOSED TRIP TO OUR MALAYSIAN CAMPS
OCTOBER 2006

Dear Fellow Veteran

I was so pleased that all who attended our 50th Reunion in Peebles on the 15th of September thoroughly enjoyed what was a unique and memorable gathering in honour of the late Josh White.

Our Guest of honour, Mr John Cushion of Malaysia Airlines, kindly presented 2 airline tickets to the winners of our Special Prize draw for the Gurkha Welfare Trust (Scottish Branch). Mr and Mrs Jim Roberts of Dalbeattie will soon be winging their way to Malaysia to visit old haunts of 50 years ago.

John has never in his lifetime experienced the warmth, comradeship and interest in Malaysia that was prevalent on that special evening. He has been in contact with me since and would like so much to give you an opportunity to revisit some of your old Camps in Malaysia.

We are therefore planning a very special, highly competitively priced package consisting of Airline Tickets, First Class Hotels and Air-conditioned busses, to give you a "Trip of a Lifetime" to that wonderful country. John has been with Malaysia Airlines for well over 20 years and has wide experience of travelling in the modern Malaysia and is able to "open doors" for our benefit.

To take advantage of this special offer will undoubtedly require some feed back from yourselves. I have, therefore, enclosed a detailed form, which will allow me to establish the demand for such a trip. Please complete the form and return it to me no later than the end of November to confirm your interest.

It will be important that you hold a current passport, full travel- and cancellation insurance and are medically fit to travel.

Don't miss this exciting opportunity and, please, inform all our Malayan Veterans who were not at Peebles as they may also wish to join us.

Yours sincerely

Ogilvie Dickson

P.S.

I am delighted to inform you that due to your immense generosity, the draw raised £1,839.40 for the Gurkha Welfare Trust. After all expenses were paid, and adding donations, we were left with a surplus of £1,789.60. Two thirds will be donated to the K.O.S.B. Association and one third to my local Melrose Branch of the Royal British Legion, all for Charitable work.

My grateful thanks to you all

Lt Col (Rtd) Shahrir Hashim, Ex Royal 5th Malaya Regiment, marching along Princes Street, Edinburgh with me on the last parade of our regiment before amalgamation with the Royal Regiment of Scotland. Friday 23rd June 2006.

Brigadier Frank Coutts receiving a ceremonial Malaysian Kris from
Lt Col Shahrir Hashim at Redford Barracks at the end of the parade.
Lt Col Hashim, Major General J Cooper DSO MBE, The King's Own Scottish Borderers, Brigadier Allan Alstead CBE,
Lt Col Donald Lear, Latifa Hashim and Brigadier Frank Coutts CBE DL.

KOSB Malayan Veterans' 2006 Trip to Malaysia

How could I refuse Malaysian Airlines' special ticket offer for my fellow veterans? Within a very brief period I had bookings from 72 veterans, 39 wives and partners, 2 escorts, 1 nurse, 1 journalist and 3 members of BBC Scotland TV News Team, with an average age of our veterans of about 70, the eldest being 88.

To take such a group on a 17,000 mile trip to the other side of the world, on a visit never before attempted, must have been one of my greatest challenges. I had no yardstick to establish costs and no past experience to rely on!

Planning commenced immediately after the Peebles event in September 2005 and I was still working on the plans when I left for Newcastle on the 22nd August 2006, to board a ferry to Holland, joining Punjab Senator, my container ship at Rotterdam bound for Singapore.

My shipmate Major Alastair Hewat, KOSB, volunteered to join me to form the advance party and our crew consisted of 7 Germans, 4 Russians and 11 Kiribati. This was my third trip to Singapore on almost identical ships, carrying well over 4,500 containers. It was also the smoothest, with only a slightly angry sea as we entered the Indian Ocean.

By now we had received a telex 'News Sheet' informing us that Singapore streets had been swept, buildings spruced up and thousands of additional flowers planted, but we discovered that this was not for Alistair and me arriving, but for the 16,000 delegates attending the annual meetings of the International Monetary Fund and World Bank Group.

As we were now off India and behind schedule, I asked the captain to try and book us into The Swissotel, explaining that I would be bringing over 100 of our group for five days. However, they wouldn't accept our booking without a credit card number! This was then sent to our shipping agent in Singapore, who inadvertently sent it to our ship's head office in Germany, and before all the faxes, emails and telexes had informed the world of my credit card number, our rooms had gone! We started all over again with the almost impossible task of finding beds. Eventually we met with success at a hotel in the Mount Elizabeth area.

However, all was not good news, full rack rate plus $50 surcharge to increase their profits during the IMF Conference, +10% service charge, +1% Gov charge, +5% GST!

However, I always look for that 'Silver Lining' and in this case our London agent estimated and charged us for 19 days' sailing time from Rotterdam to Singapore. We were actually 23 days at sea, but this unconventional travel system did not charge us for the additional 4 days of sailing, accommodation and superb food, prepared by our Russian cook! Some you win and some you lose!

On my regular visit to the bridge, I glance at the map on the chart table and I quickly forget profit and loss, as I find we are just passing Banda Aceh in Sumatra devastated by that horrendous Tsunami last year. It makes one realise the incredible power of the sea!

We have had a strong wind on our stern all the way from the tip of Sri Lanka and find that we have made a slight saving on the 165 tons of fuel oil our ship normally burns in a day.

On my nightly brisk walk round our 294m (960-foot) ship, I panicked a little as they had fixed the gratings over the stairways to prevent pirates gaining access to our cabins (I thought I would have to sleep on the deck!) Fortunately, they left the port side free for my return! I note from the bridge today: 23 pirate attacks off Bangladesh area and 43 in the Somalia area, which we passed last week. This is certainly now a major problem at sea!

VOY.NO. 044E - HJ-Charter PDS

CERTIFICATE

FOR A SEAVOYAGE ON BOARD
MS „PUNJAB SENATOR" DQVK
MR. DICKSON, Ogilvie
From Hamburg to Singapore with = 8.768 nm
WITH ALL OUR BEST WISHES FOR HEALTH
AND HAPPINESS FOR YOU AND YOUR FAMILY.

Sometimes we're looking like this print- dark and undedected. But we're available, fast ,reliable and safe. according to our ISM-Certificate .
Our sign is a well trained crew and a high standard of navigational , safety and technical equipment.

CAPT. D. Walther
AND CREW

P.Klang, the 18th of Sept. 2006

Our ship's captain takes piracy very seriously!

It's barbecue and party time on the high seas. Here I am congratulating our cook Alexander Pavlov from Russia on his imaginative food, along with my shipmate Major Alastair Hewat in high spirits, as he joins in the fun!

By the time we reached Singapore after 23 days at sea, a break of three days was most welcome, but by now we had received the sad news that Brigadier Frank Coutts and 2 other veterans couldn't make the trip due to ill health and our final figure was 69 veterans, 37 wives and partners, 2 escorts, 1 journalist and 3 members of BBC Scotland TV News Team. After a seven hour train journey on ancient rolling stock from Singapore to Kuala Lumpur, we were ready to welcome our group complete with three first class coaches.

Lt Col Ahmad Fareed bin Ariffin, Commanding Officer of Royal 5th Malaya Regiment, his wife and his R.S.M. welcoming our group at Kuala Lumpur airport on the 4th October 2006.

The outstanding backdrop provided by the Shangri La Hotel, Kuala Lumpur, for our special reception.

The Hunting Ogilvie tartan contrasts with the colourful dresses of the local dancers at a spectacular cultural show provided by our tour company after dinner in Kuala Lumpur.

The wives and partners who so loyally supported our group.

The veterans in front of Kuala Lumpur's quite dramatic war memorial, the most impressive in the Orient.

Friday the 6th October 2006

The presentation of the Pingat Jasa Malaysian medal by the Malaysian Secretary General Dato Latffi to 35 members of our group, at a special reception in the Shangri La Hotel, Kuala Lumpur, attended by a large number of local dignitaries including 8 from the Malaysian Government.

Proud to be wearing the PJM as Dato Latffi turns to pick up the next medal for John Nichol.
The event was covered by 11 members of the Malaysian press and 4 TV companies.

I was delighted to meet Gen (Rtd) Tan Sri (DR) Hashim Mohd Ali, Royal 5th Malaya Regiment and the highest ranking officer in Malaysia associated with our regiment, the King's Own Scottish Borderers.

Pipers and drummers of the Royal 5th Malaya Regiment entertain us after the presentation.

Col Paul Edwards, Defence Adviser; Self; Latifa Hashim; Brigadier Allan Alstead; Joey Edwards; Lt Col (Rtd) Shahrir Hashim, Royal 5th Malaya Regiment wearing my headgear presented to him whilst he and Latifa were the guests of Flora and me, for a week during the summer of 2006.

Kuala Lumpur to Malacca

Before we left Kuala Lumpur we remembered our lost veterans, who had planned to join us on the trip:
Drew Penman, Robert Wardhaugh and Howard McDowall.
A special service was arranged at 10.30am on Saturday 7th October and conducted by a local minister in the
Cheras Road Military Cemetery in Kuala Lumpur.
Drew's ashes were scattered and a letter from the Penman family was read by Bill Jardine from Dumfries.
A lament was played by our regimental piper John Winton.

John and Esther Crawford, reliving their honeymoon!

A new career for a retired Brigadier!

Niyor and Paloh 8th October 2006

By popular request I was able to change the entire day's itinerary with the ever-willing help of our Embassy in KL and a mobile phone as we drove from Malacca to Batu Pahat. After lunch we were on our way to that memorable visit to Niyor and Paloh.

At the famous site where Brigadier Allan Alstead contacted Brigadier Frank Coutts in Edinburgh by mobile phone and was able to give him a 'sit rep' on our trip.

They said that it was a good road to Niyor – that was until we took a shortcut through the estate and got stuck.

We made it to Niyor.

Good human relations... here Ronald Wood applies a plaster to the foot of a local who had fallen from his motorbike.

Batu Pahat 9th October 2006
The H.Q. Camp of our Regiment KOSB 1955-1958

I directed Lt Col Areffin, C.O. Royal 5th Malaya to the exact location of our camp and within minutes recruited 2 local gentlemen, one of whom could remember running messages for the camp, as a boy.

The smartly dressed veterans in the centre of Batu Pahat Camp.

Every meal was a banquet.

Highly recommended, said our tour guide, but we had to adopt unfamiliar techniques!

Kluang 9th October 2006

We will never forget the welcome extended to us by the Royal 5th Malaya Regiment, Kluang: the motorcycle outriders who escorted us from Ayer Hitam, stopping all traffic at every set of lights to allow our three buses free passage, the welcome in the hangar at Kluang Garrison, the wonderful family welcome at Royal 5th Malaya 3 Mile Camp on the Mersing Road Kluang and the spectacular Drill Parade and Beating Retreat on the Barrack Square. It was indeed an event quite beyond words.

Greeted by the officers' wives at Royal 5th Malaya H.Q.

A hand of friendship at Kluang Garrison.

Precision Drill.

A Family Gathering.

Yong Pen – Pekan Nanas and Kelapa Sawit

Niyor, Pekan Nanas and Kelapa Sawit were not on our original itinerary, but with our wonderful Reliance team we made it to each and everyone!

In the old pineapple country of Pekan Nanas.

Yong Peng.

Kelapa Sawit.

Immaculately dressed Regimental Piper John Winton did us proud at every formal occasion.

Kota Tinggi

The Jungle Training School and on to Singapore

I have never been as close as a metre from a real lion, who clawed my bag, fortunately not me!

The KOSB dog handlers with the Malaysian dog handlers.

Robert Logan looks concerned (no wonder) as he was being hugged by a real snake.

A unique historical conference between Singapore University history students, their Professor Brian Farrell and volunteers from our group discussing the Emergency with the students who were studying this part of Malaysian history.

Ogilvie Dickson, Daniel Finlay, Campbell Bunyan and John Winton were present at 8.30am on Saturday the 2nd March 1957 when His Excellency Sir Robert Black KCMG OBE Governor and Commander-in-Chief of Singapore unveiled the Singapore Memorial to officers and men of the Land and Air Forces of the Commonwealth.

ORDER OF CEREMONY

AT THE

UNVEILING OF

THE SINGAPORE MEMORIAL

TO OFFICERS AND MEN OF THE
LAND AND AIR FORCES OF THE COMMONWEALTH

BY

HIS EXCELLENCY
SIR ROBERT BLACK
K.C.M.G., O.B.E.
GOVERNOR AND COMMANDER-IN-CHIEF
OF
SINGAPORE

SATURDAY, 2ND MARCH, 1957, AT 8.30 A.M.

Evie from Reliance in Kuala Lumpur and I arranged the entire trip by email. This was a totally new experience for me, having to master the use of a computer and produce reams and reams of the printed word.

Evie Oh, Operations Manager par excellence, Reliance Sightseeing.

Helen Goh, Director of Marketing (next to me) and Jessie Toh second left and their superb team.

We all appreciated the professional service and the courteous manner in which all queries were dealt with! Reliance staff went well beyond the call of duty. They were, in fact, quite outstanding!

Walter Scott and Ogilvie Dickson.
Walter Scott originally from Dinley Farm, Liddesdale.
Have we changed that much?
Together we played, attended school,
and served in Malaya.
50 years later we returned to
visit our old camp sites together.

Ian Fraser, John McClymont, Andy Ritchie, John Nichol, Andy Anderson, Ogilvie Dickson.
We all trained together at Berwick prior to going to Malaya.

Singapore

Back to where it all started.
In front of the Officers' Mess, Selerang Garrison, Singapore.

What better place for the final dinner of our tour as the 'Long Bar Steakhouse'
at Raffles, one of the most famous hotels in the world.

The Sunday Church Parade at Orchard Road Presbyterian Church, Singapore.

A proud moment: being presented with 'The History of Changi' by the
Changi Museum Director, Mr A Jeyathurai, with Professor Brian Farrell on
the right who presented me with his book on WWII.

Farewell Singapore

Our farewell party in the Swissotel, Singapore, with our veterans' choir in full song!

17th October 2006
Michael Tinne surveys the scene at Changi Airport as the group books in for the return flight home.

We were privileged to have James Galbreath, Cameron Buttle and Dennis Kearsly from BBC Scotland TV News Team in Glasgow accompany us on this unique and historical visit.

Major Alastair Hewat and I were about to board Peking Senator in Singapore Harbour, bound for Le Havre France, and then home to Scotland, when a fax arrived from Brigadier Allan Alstead in Edinburgh. Part of the content of the fax...

'It simply could not have been better!'

What fitting words to end a quite remarkable visit.

I had the privilege to organise this unique adventure for the following . . .

Alan Rutherford & Helen, Edinburgh
Albert Thomas & Miriam, Stranraer
Albert Younger & Isabella, Jedburgh
Alex Bell & Elizabeth, Newtown St Boswells
Alex Cranston, Livingston
Alex Ritchie & Carl, Dundee (Escorts)
Andrew Whannel, Irvine, Ayrshire
Andy Anderson & Olive, Eastriggs, Annan
Andy Ritchie & Kathleen, Dundee
Arthur Haining, Glencaple, Dumfries
Bert Houston, Dumfries
(Freelance Journalist & Broadcaster)
Bill Cooper, Huddersfield (Selkirk)
Billy McColm & Jennifer, Hawick (Cameronian)
Brigadier Allan Alstead, Edinburgh
Cameron Buttle, Selkirk
(Senior Journalist BBC Scotland)
Campbell Bunyan & Valerie, Selkirk
Colin Turnbull & Louvain, Mellville, Western Australia
Crawford Jarret, Borgue, Kirkcudbright
Daniel Finlay, Glasgow
David McCrindle, Kirkmahoe, Dumfries
Dennis Kearsley, Edinburgh
(Sound Engineer BBC Scotland)
Donald Fairgrieve & Pat, St Boswells
Edgar McMinn & Audrey, Dumfries
George Borthwick & Margaret, Edinburgh
George Campbell, Kirkcudbright
George Kerr, Clovenfords, Galashiels
George Spence & Margie, Irvine, Ayrshire
George Wright, Jedburgh
Glen Graham & Margaret, Dumfries
Gordon Wilson, Galashiels
Henry Lundie & Elizabeth, Kilwinning, Ayrshire
Henry Stein, Aldershot
Ian Dow, Ormiston, East Lothian
Ian Fraser, Foyers, Inverness
Ian Johnston, Selkirk
Jack Benson & Irene, Castle Douglas
James Anderson & Catherine, Newton Stewart

James Galbreath, Linlithgow
(Senior Cameraman BBC Scotland)
James Roberts & Nancy, Dalbeattie
Jim Goodfellow, Kelso
Jim Irving & Gladys, Eaglesfield, Lockerbie
Jim Scott & Thomasina, Earlston
Jim Selfridge, Bonnyrigg
Jim Wallace & Margaret, Hawick
Jimmy Todd, Chirnside, Berwickshire
John Crawford & Esther, Melrose
John Hardie & Rosemary, Stranraer
John McClymont & Primrose, Newton Stewart
John Nichol, Newcastleton (Copshawholm)
John Smail & Peggy, Olney, Bucks
John Torrance & Norma, Alloa
John Winton and Eleanor, Buckhaven
(Our Regimental Piper)
Laurie Barnard & Isobel, Newstead, by Melrose
Major Alastair Hewat, Lilliesleaf, Melrose
(Advance Party-Sailing from Rotterdam)
Marshall Graham, Galashiels
Mason Scott & Moira, Newtown St Boswells
Max Fraser & Agnes, Dumfries
Michael Diplacito, Lanark
Michael Tinne, London
Ogilvie Dickson, Melrose
(Advance Party – Sailing from Rotterdam)
Robert Logan and Lilian, Haddington
Ronald Wood, Edinburgh
Stan Purves & Moira, Galashiels
Tom Douglas, Hawick
Tom Irvine, Dumfries
Tom Johnstone & Amy, Walkerburn, Peebles
Tom Mann, Galashiels
Viv Sharp & Elizabeth, Hawick (Our Vocalist-Poet)
Walter Scott, Rowanburn, Canonbie
Watson Brown & Janet, Penpont, Dumfries
William Jardine, Dumfries
William Watt, Roslin, Midlothian
William Whalen & Agnes, Palnackie
Willie McKie & Dorothy, Kirkcudbright

Relax

I hope you have found my book of interest and that time has allowed you to turn over the pages in comparative comfort, just like the couple I framed in Verona, Italy, and the relaxed gentleman in Changi Village, Singapore, complete with his money bag under his shirt and his cat.

Elvis Presley once said 'Life is a precious opportunity'.
I am very humble and indeed grateful for being allowed to enjoy such a variety of quite unique opportunities.